Aeolian Harp

Gunnar Bucht

Aeolian Harp

An Essay Concerning the Nature of Tone

PETER LANG

Frankfurt am Main · Berlin · Bern · Bruxelles · New York · Oxford · Wien

Bibliographic Information published by the Deutsche Nationalbibliothek
The Deutsche Nationalbibliothek lists this publication in the Deutsche Nationalbibliografie; detailed bibliographic data is available in the internet at http://dnb.d-nb.de.

With the support of
the Sven and Dagmar Salén Foundation.

English translation: Roger Tanner.

Cover Design and Illustration:
© Olaf Gloeckler, Atelier Platen, Friedberg

ISBN 978-3-631-63575-9
© Peter Lang GmbH
Internationaler Verlag der Wissenschaften
Frankfurt am Main 2012
All rights reserved.

All parts of this publication are protected by copyright. Any utilisation outside the strict limits of the copyright law, without the permission of the publisher, is forbidden and liable to prosecution. This applies in particular to reproductions, translations, microfilming, and storage and processing in electronic retrieval systems.

www.peterlang.de

To the memory of Jacques Handschin

Contents

Preliminaries 9
Tone and Sound 11
Tone and Myth 31
Tone and Space 45
Tone and Music 79
Tone and Meaning 103
References 113
Index 117

English translation: Roger Tanner
With the support of the Sven and Dagmar Salén Foundation

Preliminaries

Generally speaking, the philosophy of music hitherto can be said to approach music, as it were, from above or from outside. Music, thus envisaged, can be "absolute" or "sounding forms in motion". It can be expression, have a linguistic meaning, tell a story, be a manifestation of "the world as will and conceptualisation", mirror society's inward contradictions. Music is seen as an activity, sometimes an interactivity, not least through an anthropological approach in which prominence is given to its origins.

Over the past fifteen years I have devoted a great deal of effort to the authorship of music essays, resulting in seven books, the main emphasis of which has been on philosophical and ideo-historical aspects, with ontological approaches increasingly coming to the fore. In the course of this work a phenomenon has crystallised out as being central to an understanding of what music "really" is. That phenomenon is *tone*. Far be it from me to claim that up till now the philosophy of music has been unaware of the importance of tone for music, or that the philosophy of music as hitherto pursued lacks insights or valuable perspectives. On the contrary. But the philosophy as practised has disregarded the central importance of the tone phenomenon for all contemplation of music. The approaches mentioned above, not least in their anthropological capacity, are also applicable to phenomena other than music and are thus not particularly distinctive of music itself. The problem consists in the above mentioned top-down perspective, which obscures the uniqueness of the phenomenon itself.

The work which now follows is an attempt to reverse the argument, by taking the phenomenon of tone as the starting point to work my way up to an understanding of the phenomenon of music, to make a philosophy of tone the foundation of a philosophy of music. Such thoughts were already present in my previous works, but, being available only in Swedish, will be enlarged on here. Throughout I employ the term *tone* and not *note*, partly because the former exposes the etymological derivation from the *tonos* of classical Greek, and also because the latter unnecessarily confines the phenomenon to the notion of music put down in writing.

Tone and Sound

"Are tones tones or are they Webern?" was the question once asked by John Cage at a seminar during the famous Darmstadt International Summer Courses for New Music. For several years the music of Anton Webern was at the centre of attention on these courses, and that music is of course distinguished by its concentration on the single tone. Or rather, the musical process is split into a series of tones separated by pauses for which the term "point music" or "punctualism" was minted. Cage's question can be taken as challenging the notion of a certain style of music setting the norm for one's view of the tone phenomenon. But it can still more be construed as a plaidoyer for the freedom of tone and – ultimately – the freedom of sound. Cage's piano composition *4'33"* exemplifies this. The pianist enters, walks up to the piano, bows to the audience, sits down and opens the lid, and then sits still without touching the keys. First silence prevails, then after a time other sounds are heard, such as the creaking of a chair, coughs from the audience, the faint whir of the air conditioning and so on. After four minutes and thirty-three seconds the pianist closes the lid, bows to the audience and exits, presumably to the accompaniment of scattered applause. We heard the "real" sounds, but are left to imagine the sounds from the piano.

This is exactly the point which Cage is out to make – drawing our attention to what we usually don't notice, luring us, through the concert situation and its pre-programmed requirement of intense listening, into an unfamiliar situation in which, as Cage puts it, we can find ourselves "happy new ears". The sounds are meant to be as interesting to us and as deserving of study as any tones by Webern. In principle, then, there is no difference between tone and sound – both are equally deserving of great attention and appear replete with meaning.

The same observation was made by the French author and recording engineer Pierre Schaeffer, who, while working for RTF at the end of the 1940s, came to ponder the artistic possibilities latent in new technology in the form of gramophone records and recorded tapes. He must also have been struck by the similarity between "listening in" and the educational method ascribed to Pythagoras, who lectured and tutored his pupils from behind a screen or drape, so that the pupils could not see him but still heard him – as was presumably his intention – hearing him better than if they had also seen him and thus been distracted, perhaps beginning to wonder about his body language or apparel. The Greeks had a word for that kind of situation: *akousma*, "that which is heard" but – by implication – "is not seen". Opinions may differ concerning the efficacy of this teaching method, but, leaving that issue aside, let us concentrate instead on the situation by which Schaeffer was confronted: the potential of the new technical media and the new listener situation, its "acousmatic" character.

Schaeffer's deliberations resulted in the phenomenon which he termed *musique concrète* and which meant that not only the traditionally musical sounds of voice and instrument but *all* sounds, even those in our everyday surroundings, could be used as artistic material. One early manifestation of this view was *Étude aux chemins de fer*, in which Schaeffer employed sounds recorded in a shunting yard: a steam locomotive, whistle sounding, slowly starts a puffing which then accelerates more and more, the bump of joins in the rails, the screech of wagons or carriages over the points, and so on. Other titles in the same direction are a joint production by Schaeffer and Pierre Henry: *Symphonie pour un homme seul* and Henry's *Variations sur une porte et un soupir*.

One is struck by the way in which these titles underline the origin of the works in traditional music – etude, symphony, variation – and this is no coincidence. Schaeffer claims that *musique concrète* is a new offshoot of the tree of music, while at the same time he is at great pains to persuade us to experience it in essentially the same way as older, more familiar music. Thus he constructs a music theory, *Solfège*, and a theoretical/analytical superstructure entitled *Traité des objets musicaux*. Here he builds up a systemisation of listening round every conceivable sound, from the most "concrete" to the most esoteric/abstract, from thick to thin, from rough to smooth. The consistent theme is the equation of all sounds, whether appearing as tones or noises, and getting us to perceive them as legitimate material for artistic creation, for composition. The problem with "concrete" sounds such as train noises, the splash of water, falling trees, squeaky doors, is that they have an extraordinarily powerful "anecdotal" character, i.e. that one has no difficulty identifying the source of the sound and is thus immediately able to infer what in a traditional sense is an extra-musical happening, an anecdote. The train noise testifies to a train rushing onwards, not a sound or timbre with an intrinsic value. Schaeffer seeks to overcome this difficulty with his music theory, his aim being to generalise the structure of sounds, to condition our mode of perception so that we will get out of the habit of hearing a train as a train, instead of hearing it as music.

This is the exact opposite of the situation in traditional programme music: in Arthur Honegger's symphonic poem *Pacific 231* we hear the orchestra imitating the hissing of the steam engine and its initial puffing, the train getting off to a jerky start the gradually increasing speed. The music wants to tell a story, wants to have the character of anecdote and at the same time to keep its character of "pure" music. *Étude aux it Chemins de Fer*, by contrast the author begins with the anecdote but wants us to forget it. In *Traité* he draws a comparison to the tone from a violin: hearing such a tone, we seldom if ever give a thought to its being produced with the aid of horsehair and a gut string. All we hear is the result, without any hint of anecdote, and we listen in to expression.

Schaeffer's *Traité* is a voluminous work with an elaborate typology. Since its publication in the 1960s, others have gone on to develop and refine the description and systematisation of sounding objects, a matter which, however, comes outside the scope of this present account. On the other hand it is interesting to ask whether Schaeffer succeeds in his bid to de-anecdotalise concrete sounds, to make them function as sounds with an intrinsic value, as music. In a word, he does not seem to have. We still experience everyday sounds as evidence of and signals from everyday sounds; and nothing can change our minds on that score. In that particular respect, Schaeffer seems to have got it wrong. But "accidents of history" have resulted in the outlines of a new art, acousmatics, which is further developing both the listener situation and the sounding raw material and its processing.

What, briefly, are the distinguishing characteristics of this new art? First and foremost, it is a further development of the electro-acoustic music whose principal tools are recording tape and loudspeakers and whose roots are to be found both with Schaeffer and his circle and in the Cologne electronic music studio of the 1950s. Furthermore: "Acousmatic art definitely ranks among the 'fine arts', whereas instrumental and vocal music belongs exclusively to the 'performing arts' category" (Bodin). In other words, what we hear is a series of sound pictures which are not necessarily interconnected. The situation resembles that of pictorial art: one walks or browses from picture to picture, with the experienced moment at the centre of attention. The picture is stationary, even when sounding. Acousmatic art is rooted in music but has left the nest and established itself as an independent phenomenon.

Let us now put man's experience of the acoustic world around him at the centre of attention. That world, of course, varies from one epoch or region to another, and it is hard to recreate within ourselves the acoustic landscapes of times past. Even so, such documentation does exist, and a brilliant example of a historical soundscape brought to life can be found in the opening chapter of August Strindberg's novel *The Red Room*, published in 1879. We hear the different pitches and timbres of the various church bells mingling to form a veritable symphony of the city, played out in a large visual space. We also hear another sound, namely the twittering of small birds – "What a life it was!" A depiction like that can serve as a pilot into our own acoustic landscape, alerting us to that which we actually hear – not just church bells, but also traffic noise, sounds from worksites, people and animals. A city environment sounds quite different from the countryside, where the silence is punctuated by the odd tractor, the distant barking of a dog or bleating sheep and, depending on the time of year, birdsong. To which are added human voices – speaking, shouting, singing, conversing. Coexisting with these sounds on a parity basis, we have for example sirens, foghorns, car hooters and voltage. Then again, one finds certain animal sounds manifested as tones, e. g. from whales, beef cattle and, above all, birds. These last mentioned have inspired mankind to imitate them, not least as in music like Beethoven's *Pastorale*, Wagner's *Siegfried* and Messiaen's *Oiseaux exotiques*. All in all, we find that tone is a vital component of the aggregate world of sound, included in it as one category among others. And yet, through no fault of its own, so to speak, it has come to occupy a very special position. How can this be? Why is it experienced as something *sui generis*? The answer lies in man's capacity for transcendence, for reaching beyond the obvious. But before stepping that far we have to ask ourselves: what is a tone – really?

One good rule of thumb when addressing such an essentialist issue is to ponder the word/term itself and its etymology. The word derives from the Greek *tonos*, meaning "tension" or "that which is stretched", which immediately puts in mind of a tensed, vibrant string or vocal cord. The latter is indeed illustrative, pointing as it does to the difference between tone and pitch. It was already observed by Aristoxenus, a pupil of Aristotle's, that song and speech have pitch in common, and the human voice confirms this. When speaking, we change the pitch of our voices all the time, but if, in the midst of speech, we break into song, we linger at a specific pitch and maintain it. We have a feeling of the throat being constricted and the vocal cords consequently vibrating. In speech we modulate, in song we focus. In short: *tone requires focus*.

This statement needs to be refined. Switching from speech to song is like moving from one world to another. At the same time the transition is emphasised as a consequence of focus, with the production of a tone the essential consideration. But focus can also be applied to listening. Every time we settle down in our seats in a concert hall to listen to an orchestral concert, we experience a ritual with a purpose: the orchestra tuning up. The fugleman is the first oboist, whose one-line *a* sets the norm. This event is preceded by the silence of the orchestra, and out of that silence is born the tone to which all must relate. It is a tone endowed with an aura and its character is rich in promise: things are going to happen here. And indeed they do, for soon afterwards a veritable chaos erupts – the autonomous tootlings of the players. One tone gives birth to other tones, one single tone triggers all the other tones. The tone as a magic point.

Having come this far, we must pause to reflect on what has now been said. The tuning tone of the oboe has a standing among the sounds of the concert hall resembling that of the tone in the acoustic world around us. It has a very special character which attracts our attention. The sounding sounds also attract our attention, but that attention is of a different kind. The tone has two functions: to be the fixed point of our attention while at the same time being able to signal a process, an event or an action. The sound, by contrast, has a signalling function only, informing us of events in the world around us, and is an important instrument in a strategy of survival. The sound is the overarching category of which the tone forms part. In other words, all tones are sounds, but not all sounds are tones.

The difference between tone and sound can also be expressed in acoustic terms. Sound reaches us through vibrations in the air, but these vibrations or waves are irregular by nature, cross over each other and, observed by oscillograph, convey an amorphous impression. Tone is a different case: the atmospheric oscillation by which tone is carried has a certain length containing a number of smaller fluctuations. The big fluctuation or sound wave is regular, whereas the small ones present a steadily diminishing length, referred to as overtones. These latter have tended to be seen as the reason for certain tone combinations being preferred to others, as a prototype of both triads and the creation of tonal systems, but this is contradicted by our experiencing overtones, not as separate but as lumped together, a phenomenon called tone colour which, together with the actual onset of the tone, is extremely important for tonal experience. But they are a by-product which cannot conceivably exist independently of the sound wave by which it is generated. A tone cannot be reduced to its physical/acoustic prerequisites but has to be experienced in order to be properly understood.

How do we perceive a tone? This question occupied scientists and philosophers, not only in the ancient world but also in more modern times, at least from the mid-19th century onwards. Hermann von Helmholtz and Carl Stumpf, Wolfgang Köhler and Erich von Hornbostel, Franz Brentano and Hugo Riemann are leading names in this connection, but so too perhaps are persons taking a more passing interest in the matter, such as Charles Darwin, Herbert Spencer and Edmund Gurney. Their contributions to a history of ideas concerning tone serve to illustrate the tangled nature of the subject, the multiplicity of conflicting opinions and, sometimes, a muddiness of presentation. (For a closer study, the reader is referred to Michael Maier's *Jacques Handschin's "Toncharakter"*, published in 1991). Certain keywords nonetheless crystallise out as vital *points d'appui* for an understanding of the problem, namely pitch, tone quality, timbre, interval, consonance and amalgamation. Essentially, the discussion centres round these phenomena and their interrelationships. One can also reflect on the protagonists' backgrounds. Remarkably many of them are non-musicians – not just Spencer and Darwin, but Brentano, Helmholtz and Köhler too. This ties in with a philosophical tradition whereby music is looked on as an exceedingly interesting topic of study, a tradition which we must consider wholly commendable. Every cultural manifestation benefits from being illuminated from outside, and at best the perspective can be both sharpened and nuanced in this way.

The expression "history of tone theory" has been used to denote thinking on the subject of tone from Aristoxenos to Hermann von Helmholtz onwards. With von Helmholtz a period begins during which tone is explored through analysis, observations and experimentation. This scientific method is typical, not least, of Helmholtz, to whom overtones become a central category. This perspective is reiterated by Stumpf, who adds to it a psychological approach. Both these approaches are opposed by musicologist, linguist and organist Jacques Handschin in his *Der Toncharakter*, published in 1948. His perspective is neither scientific nor psychological but philosophical/historical. Like the specialist he is in medieval music, with profound insights into the musical culture of the ancient world, he sets about filling the gap between Aristoxenos and Helmholtz in the history of ideas and formulating alternatives to the positivist method on a number of points. For example, where Helmholtz allots the overtone phenomenon a central role in accounting for consonance, Handschin points out that we hear overtones, not as tones but as timbre. Where Stumpf dismantles, atomises tone, Handschin holds onto it as "this and none other". Where Stumpf dismantles the properties of tone, Handschin compares them. Where Stumpf distinguishes between quality and non-quality, Handschin distinguishes between centre and periphery. His next step is to enquire after something still more pivotal than pitch and to combine this with the sustaining of "tone". To this he contrasts timbre and intensity (volume), which are the changeable elements and thus impart character to the tone. In this way attention is made to focus on the "still more pivotal". The sustained tone attracts its various character opportunities and imparts musical content to the conceptual differences, points to "this other".

Handschin's approach is synthetic, not analytical. He emphasises the wholeness of our experience of tone, its musical character. As I see it, this is a fruitful perspective, something which I have endeavoured to show in my *Quid est tonus?* Hence the argument which now follows will take Handschin's thoughts as its jumping-off point, proceeding from their to my own conclusions.

Handschin begins with the question of tone and its properties. Right here he makes a statement concerning the essence of music, taking issue with those who maintain that *one* tone is not music, that several tones are needed. Even though he concedes that a tone assumes true musical properties only when included as a member of a larger tonal world, logically speaking, the tone is music's basic building block. An ordered tonal sequence, a melody, bears within it a number of building blocks which assume the melody's property of music, are musically coloured by it and become music.

Polemicising against earlier tone psychologists, i. e. those whose views have just been hinted at, he maintains that a tone is inseparable from its properties, that it is an object, something concrete and given. As a precursor he makes reference to the 16th century theorist Gioseffo Zarlino, who reflected on musical objects, which he termed *soggetto*. If Handschin (d. 1955) had had a sporting chance, he could also have invoked the father of *musique concrète*, Pierre Schaeffer, who, as we have already seen, coined the terms sounding and musical object respectively. Be this is as it may, to Handschin tone is a concrete object with certain properties. What properties?

The answer to this question has in fact already been given: pitch, timbre and intensity, to which are added the duration of the tone, its length. These latter three properties are aspects of one and the same tone, "peripheral" in relation to the central position of pitch. But then Handschin goes on to ask whether there might not be a property which is still more than pitch for describing a tone. He is by no means alone in doing so: tone psychology has attempted to find the property inherent in the tone itself, from which the term "tonicity" (*Tonigkeit*), for example, has been coined – a somewhat diffuse property, but betokening an insight into tone being more than pitch, of its having certain musical properties. Without in this context mentioning Aristoxenos's distinction between pitch and tone – with which he is of course acquainted – Handschin here introduces *separate pitches*, meaning tones sounding higher or lower, sharper or softer. He places the tones in their "society" and asks whether this still more pivotal entity could not be found in this community. Here the phenomenon of consonance assumes a pivotal role, as is already the case in earlier tone psychology, where an attempt is made to explain it with the aid of the term "fusion" (*Verschmelzung*), meaning that two tones are perceived as being close together, being almost absorbed by each other. This, however, is probably more a description of the phenomenon than an explanation of its genesis. Handschin therefore introduces the concept of the cycle of fifths, a well-known term in the theory of modulation, which, however, here assumes a different and wider significance than to the theorist and the piano tuner. Since the octave, with its in-built identity, is of no use for relating *different* tones to each other, the fifth becomes the second "best" interval, combining proximity with difference. As back-up, Handschin has an overwhelming historical experience from such widely differing music cultures as those of the Occident and China, in which both the diatonic and pentatonic scale can be constructed with the aid of what is termed generation from the fifth.

Tone character, then, is fundamentally important and is conditioned by the position of the tone in the tonal system, i. e. the cycle of fifths. The tones within this are not only members of a system but illuminate each other as neighbours, like living beings in a reciprocal relationship, like members of a family or perhaps even citizens in a society. We do not find reciprocity in the chromatic scale, where the tones are reduced to pitch only, devoid of character, perhaps an image of society's anonymity. In tone character, by contrast, a reciprocal illumination occurs, for instance when two tones follow each other or sound simultaneously, i. e. when we hear an interval. The expressions which Handschin uses to characterise tones and intervals are partly of a more general nature, such as "firm", "affirmative", "empty", "dense", "full" etc., and partly more specific, as when he says that a tone of *f*-character is one having a semitone and two whole tones under it and three whole tones plus a semitone above it, while a tone of *d*-character has whole tones and semitones etc. both below and above it. Since the tonal system is based on fifths, the tones are as far apart from each other as the number of fifth intervals.

Handschin describes the antithesis of pitch and tone character in terms of outward and inward. According to this way of seeing things, pitch is the outward property, observable by the senses, which stresses the ordering of the tones in a scale. The visual image of the scale reinforces this view. Tone character, on the other hand, is the inward, true musical property of the tone. This characterisation could be reworded using the terms "tone position" and "tone value". Handschin refers to the ancient Greeks, and above all to Pythagoras, to whom the consonances between tones were the very foundation of music and consonance its true beginning. Consonance appears to have been understood, not so much as an outward, simultaneously sounding phenomenon but rather as an inward tone relation within the sound, the close and manifest.

Clearly, Handschin had a both different and – considering the frame of reference – wider grasp than is usual in more recent music philosophy. His view of music mirrors his profound familiarity with medieval and ancient music, coupled with a scepticism of the positivism of his contemporaries and their inclination to experiment. He concedes that the tone characters are most clearly apparent in homophonic music, i. e. plainsong, while on the other hand the polyphonic repertoire from early attempts to the first half of the 20th century does not allow them to be so clearly manifested. But they are there all the same, in the form of key characteristics, i. e. the notion of different keys having different characters. To this one may object that these are merely shifts of the major and minor scales within the framework of our modern tonal system, the twelve-tone chromatic scale, and that key characters are imaginary. I myself at least have previously argued along these lines, but have subsequently had a rethink, because there is no ignoring the fact of composers in the past having moved in this conceptual world and allowed it to influence their creativity, become part of their expression. Two examples will serve to illustrate this point. It is clear to me that Beethoven's and Bruckner's seventh symphonies, in A and E major respectively, are closely bound up with the choice of key in the whole of their structure, sound character and treatment of themes. Many people – composers, then, among them – attribute to these keys a radiance which infects the sounding music, or perhaps vice versa: the music derives its inspiration from the choice of key. Instead of "radiance" we could note that, starting with the middle *c* of the cycle of fifths, both keys are on what we call the dominant side, i. e. "higher up" in contrast to the opposite direction, termed *sub*dominant in music. On perhaps not wholly serious grounds, Handschin launches the expressions "female" and "male" for the dominant and subdominant sides respectively, his motive being to avoid designations excessively associated with a particular epoch or genre. Even so he gives us time-related tabs for, as it were, translating these expressions, with "female" corresponding to the light and unstable and "male" to the ponderous and stable, which can extend down to the darkly menacing. Whether these characters could be applied to the above mentioned symphonies is an open question: in addition to radiance, both works display an ecstatic touch which in Beethoven's case escalates to fury, which may have prompted Handschin himself, in his *Musikgeschichte im Überblick*, p. 350, to highlight the sometimes bellicose nature of Beethoven's music.

The question asked earlier concerning our tone experience remains supremely relevant as we now turn to consider the distance between tones, i. e. intervals, and the criteria of distance which can apply. Two views are possible, views which both contrast with each other and at the same time reinforce one another. One of them is based on generation by fifths, the other on a scale. The first method determines the distance of the tones from each other in relation to the number of fifths in between. Thus *a* and *e* are close together, in fact as close as one can get, while *e* and *f* are separated by no fewer than five fifths. The difference between a tone system based on fifths and one based on alternating whole tones and semitones, i. e. a scale, is obvious from the exemplification: the "optically" larger intervals of the fifth system become near neighbours, while the "optically" small intervals of the scale system are very far apart. Here we have two different ways of measuring tone distance and the implicit spatial experience conditioned thereby. Accustomed as we are to basing our assessment of interval size on the appearance of the tone scale – with the semitone as the smallest interval – this seems to us the most natural way of measuring tone distance, i. e. the second is a small interval while the seventh is a large one, which affects our experience of the expression. The system of fifths, on the other hand, is less obvious, because the tones in apparently small intervals can be far apart while with larger intervals the opposite tends to apply. In the first instance – taking the tone scale as the starting point – one might possibly say that the distance is determined by outward, "optical" criteria, while the second instance – with the system of fifths as the starting point – puts more emphasis on inward, more subtle criteria for judging distance and with it spatial experience. A few examples will serve to illustrate this point.

The third movement of Anton Bruckner's 9th symphony opens with a melody on the strings which is joined, in the second half of the second bar, by a chord from the brass. E major, the basic key, is here conspicuous by its absence. Instead the starting point is the tone *b-natural* followed by a minor ninth upwards, two semitones downwards and a descending octave. The melody then climbs up via fourth-semitone-whole tone-semitone, landing on one-line *g*. The largest and smallest intervals, in the conventional sense, are especially interesting here, i. e. on the one hand the ninth and octave and on the other the minor second. In the scale perspective, the distance between the tones in the opening ninth leap is very wide, which also applies to the system of fifths – no fewer than five fifths on the "male" subdominant side. The ensuing downward semitone has the same tones as the ninth leap, but in reverse order, i. e. two-line *c* – one-line *b*. From the viewpoint of the system of fifths, the distance remains unaltered, five fifths, but in reverse order, while in the scale system the distance has shrunk to the least conceivable. The same applies to the ensuing semitone *b – a#*, five fifths in the "female", dominant direction and the smallest possible distance. The octave leap which follows is interesting: in the perspective of the system of fifths, no move takes place at all, and accordingly no distance can be observed, while within the framework of the scale system the movement is considerable despite the identity of tone, in fact almost as great as the opening ninth leap, but inverted. It is as though the octave answers the ninth, borrowing its expressive force from the latter and in this way making up for the lack of any fifth remove.

Here, for the first time, we have introduced a property termed "expressive force", and we shall look more closely to see what, in the example quoted, can be said to generate that property. The basic formula seems to be: the greater the interval, the greater the expressive force. This view is nourished by the score and by the scale system in which the distance between the tones is clear for all to see. The optical induces thoughts of this kind, which does not prevent there being a good deal in them. The overcoming of a distance requires a concentration of force – you gather yourself together and take a deep breath. All this comes close to the will to expression, meaning to communicate, to reach, to bridge distances and in this way to form the space. The expression sustains the space.

From this it can be concluded that expression is founded solely on distance and overcoming thereof. This, however, is not enough, as witness the cycle of fifths, the distance criterion of which is based, not so much on optical characteristics as on inherent tone characters. Distance in itself is no sufficient criterion but must be qualitatively determined by components it includes, i.e. tones and their characters. Both distance and tone character, scale system as well as system of fifths, make a difference to expression. The manner in which they interact or counteract each other, the way in which they clash with or nuance one another, decides our experience of expression.

The fundamental importance of tone and interval for our experience of music is surely beyond doubt, and the Bruckner example underlines this. But it would be a mistake to rely solely on the importance of these phenomena for expression. The example referred to, not least, indicates other aspects too, concentrated here into timbre and intensity. The melody is presented *forte* by unison strings whose mass effect is an expressive quality in itself. To this is added the mode of execution, i. e. *vibrato* and phrasing, which heighten the expressiveness still further. These may seem truisms, but in the midst of all more or less sophisticated arguments, these aspects must also be given the place they deserve, even if, generally speaking, they are not at the centre of our attention.

Another example is provided by Béla Bartók's *Music for Strings, Percussion and Celesta*, the presentation of the fugue subject in the first movement. In this music the fifth plays a role in more ways than one. For one thing, the theme has a range – ambitus – of a fifth. Above all, the thematic entries of the fugue come in fifths in both directions, counting from the central point, i. e. the tone *a*. The "female" and "male" elements alternate, performing a kind of antiphony until they meet at the point furthest away on the cycle of fifths, namely *e- flat*. Then the music turns about and moves in both directions through the cycle of fifths until the voices meet at the opening tone of *a* with a prolonged expulsion of breath. The whole of this process is combined with a crescendo up to the furthest point, *e- flat*, which in this way becomes the climax of the *ff* nuance, only to be transformed into a diminuendo back to the *pianissimo* of the end point *a*. The "female" and "male" elements urge one another on to the orgasm of the climax, which is followed by a prolonged fading of tone. It is unlikely that either Bartók or Handschin would have appreciated this interpretation – after all, we are not talking about the overture to *Tristan and Isolde*! But Handschin at least has only himself to blame, for choosing a terminology which encourages flights of fancy.

The hard core of this argument is that the system of fifths functions in a new and unexpected way relevant to the overarching course of the music. But what do things look like in miniature, in the actual fugue subject's interval distribution? The melody in the example is made up of semitones, minor thirds and whole tones. No other interval occurs. Here too, of course, one could apply the system of fifths to the judgement of distance and find that the tones included in the semitone interval are furthest away from each other while in the case of the whole-tone interval the opposite applies: the constituent tones are closest together. But here the scale system seems to take command of our assessment of the intervals. We experience them primarily as constricted and the melody as constantly falling back to the point of departure, describing circles round itself. (A Swedish reviewer opined that the music was reminiscent of a can of wriggling worms!). The timbre also contributes to the expression: the melody is played by two violas *con sordino*.

The third and last example is taken from the opening of Richard Wagner's *Parsifal* and, more specifically, the unison melody with which the overture begins. This is music I have returned to on any number of occasions and which, moreover, Handschin quotes as an example of ingenious harmonic thinking (*Der Toncharakter* p. 292). I would like to briefly recapitulate my reflections on this melody, while at the same time adding it to the discussion concerning the relation between the scale system and the system of fifths. Even though the harmonic dimension is implicitly there, concentration on the melodic is the distinguishing factor, as witness the reduction of the rhythmic elements – with one exception – to giving each constituent tone a different note value from its immediate predecessor, a reduction which enables the melody to blossom forth. In this way it comes quite close to being a richly ornate Gregorian melody, and arguably it moves in the Lydian mode, using both *b-natural* and *b-flat* – though here transposed to *a-flat*-tonality and the corresponding tones *d* and *d-flat*. The final tone, the prolonged, fading *c*, reinforces the modal impression while at the same time echoing what Handschin declared the "ingenious" *c-minor* "intonation" in bar 3, within *A-flat major*.

This raises the aspect which the system of fifths offers, with the tone *a-flat* as the starting point. We then find that all tones but one are between one and six steps on the dominant side, indeed one of them even seven fifth steps, i. e. tritone and the tone *d*. The exception is the tone *d-flat*, positioned on the first fifth step on the subdominant side. Recalling the "superior" position of the dominant in relation to that of the subdominant, and considering that in the course of the drama the melody is divided into various leitmotifs,

i. e. that it can be said to contain a concentration of the expressive character, we could argue that the emphasis on the "right" or "female" might possibly have to do with the basic theme of the composition: compassion and reconciliation.

The melody, then, has distinctly modal traits, at the same time as there is no mistaking its major and minor character. In this way it deftly conjoins with the scale system, thus forming a happy synthesis with the system of fifths. With reference to the gestic, and with the previous examples also included, one could essay the following characterisation: Bruckner excels in grand gestures and one can be put in mind of a preacher or actor tasked with convincing the audience and making an impression on them. With Bartók we seem to have a lecturer standing there and mumbling to himself, introverted and oblivious of his surroundings. Wagner, on the other hand, fashions a restrained eloquence which savours the words in the same way as the melody seems to savour the different tone characters, lingering on them, gently caressing them and in this way refining them. The mixed sound – strings and woodwinds – cause tone colour as such to defer to pitch, tone character and, consequently, tone. The music and its tones hover freely, giving us a hint of what *Musik an sich* might be.

We have dwelt a great deal on *the distance* between tones and its expressive implications. Our experience of tone depends on the existence of a tone continuum from the lowest to the highest audible. From this continuum we pick out certain fixed points, pitches. In between them, silence prevails. Let us for a moment imagine music without fixed pitches. The sounding result would be what is called *glissando*, i. e. a perpetual slithering up and down of pitch within the confines of audibility. Pitch is indeed the starting point, but it is a pitch that is constantly giving way, whereupon a species of musical seasickness can occur in the listener and, continuing the train of thought, even affect his or her sense of balance. We would comprehend both space and movement, but very bleakly, without the wealth of nuance and, sometimes, drama distinguishing the combination of distinct pitches and intervals. Of course, a glissando, properly inserted, can be highly effective, as for example with certain styles of playing in the Viennese performance tradition or sections of music by Bartók and Xenakis or even later composers. In cases of that kind, the glissando enriches the playing of delimited tones and intervals, reminding us that there is a world behind them, a dark, amorphous world which, without being absorbed by the everyday world of sound, somewhere challenges, indeed parodies, the world of tones and all that it stands for.

To further clarify this point, i. e. what tones stand for, the tonal world will once again be related to the world of sound, without anticipating too much of the discussion to follow. Here, then, we are confronted by two very different acoustic worlds. The more comprehensive of them, the world of sound, is something we live with day and night, something which accompanies and governs our everyday existence. As has already been remarked, it also includes tones, or rather pitches, which, but only under very special conditions, are transformed into tones with character. This situation arises when a person listens to them and in his or her brain transforms them, gives them meaning, creates a world of tones. That world organises our auditive perception in a way which is meaningful, full of meanings. We create for ourselves a sounding antipicture to that which is given. People in other and earlier music cultures have been aware of this. The late-classical philosopher Boethius, for example, writes of *musica mundana, musica humana* and *musica instrumentalis*. Leaving aside for a moment the question of what Boethius means by these terms, I would like here to test an interpretation relevant to what has been said so far. The first term, "the world's music", would be the world of sound about us, including the occurrence of distinct pitches. In short, the acoustic prerequisites of anything sounding in the first place. The second term, "human music", indicates man's capacity for converting pitch into tone and character – in short, a living tone with meaning. Tone perception is, as the expression sometimes goes, an anthropotypical property, humanly universal. The third term, "music of instruments", alludes to the wealth of variation from one music culture to another, which tones are chosen and how they are grouped into very different scales reflecting the ethnotype, that which distinguishes people within each culture.

This interpretation has something in common with what Boethius is referring to, namely *musica instrumentalis* as a collective term for the actually sounding music, that which man performs in practice. By *musica humana*, on the other hand, Boethius means the ability of music to unit body and soul in a harmonic whole. This psychophysical connection has a certain affinity to Handschin's view of what underlies the phenomenon of consonance. He takes as his starting point the well-known fact that the simpler the proportion an interval presents with regard to oscillation rate and string length, the more consonant it will be. The octave is the essence of this phenomenon, manifested in the ratio of 1 : 2 and 2 : 1. The tones are virtually identical and there is no different of tone character between them. A difference does not come until the fifth and the proportions 2 : 3 and 3 : 2. Thus the number 3 is fundamental to tone characters obtained by means of potentiation, i. e. 3 raised to the power of 1, 2 and 3 or, conversely, negative potentiation, and potentiation and its negation to the circle of fifths in, respectively, the "female" and "male" direction.

The fifth, then, next to the octave, is the simplest interval in the ratio and thus the most consonant and, accordingly, fundamental to the construction of a tone system. To Handschin and many like him, this congruence between the reality of numbers and that of our psyche is something of a miracle. In this miracle he includes the tone characters and their counterpart in the above mentioned potentiations. Not surprisingly, Pythagoras is invoked, and his experience of the inner and outer world in some mysterious way corresponding to each other. Handschin emphasises that he is speaking of the world of tones as such, without holding any brief for a particular aesthetic of music. Nevertheless, he can imagine tones, through their order, being more than material to an artist, being capable of inspiring the artist to create in harmony with this particular order whose meaning is the correspondence between outward and inward. Here we are moving towards, not only philosophy but metaphysics too. The world of tones is both an outer and inner reality and music is not an island unto itself. On the contrary, music presents itself, in a very special way, as an image of the Creation, perhaps even of the Creator?

The word "metaphysics" has just been dropped and it is nothing for us to be afraid of. We should be open to premonition and dream, for which reason, as a rejoinder to the quotation with which this chapter began, I would like to add another quotation by way of concluding vignette. Robert Schumann heads his great piano Fantasie in C major with a motto from Friedrich Schlegel which translates as follows: "Among all the sounds in earth's many-coloured dream/ One soft note calls to the secret listener". But I prefer the beauty of the original German: *"Durch alle Töne tönet im bunten Erdentraum ein leiser Ton gezogen für den der heimlich lauschet"*. Notice the word *gezogen*. Strictly speaking, it means "drawn", i. e. a tone made to sound by the drawing of a bow over a string. Could Schlegel and Schumann have had in mind Pythagoras' single-stringed monochord, *kanon* in Greek, meaning "yardstick"? If sound is the world, is tone the world's explanation?

Tone and Myth

"...Then, some friend, silent witness of our happy days of love, would with his own hands, dig us a grave at the feet of an aged oak, ... and hang upon its stretching boughs the orphaned harp, whose strings, caressed by the wind stirring the trembling leaves, would breathe its last faint harmonies unto the sighing air. Then sitting down beside our grave, that friend would recall my last song, which mingling with this funeral strain, would bring the tear of compassion to his eye, and with a shudder, he would dream of time and space, ... of love...and...oblivion...".

The speaker listens, with an expression of profound melancholy, to the music which immediately follows. We hear a *tremolo* of muted strings with growing and diminishing tone volume interspersed with the *pizzicato* of deep strings and an almost inaudible *arpeggio* from the harp. The process is repeated and varied, the harmonies are ambiguous, the music seems to be groping its way forward. Suddenly a melody on the clarinet is heard in the distance, at the same time as the harmony finds firmer ground under its feet. The melody surges and fades, as if wanting to remind us of something. The string *tremolo* and the broken chords on the harp continue in the background, the process is halted by fermata pause and time signatures implying cessation. Towards the end the music lands on a dominant seventh chord which is never resolved, the clarinet and harp disappear, leaving just the strings, now without any *tremolo*, slowly dying away in the distance with small changes of volume. The whole thing has the character of a vision with neither beginning nor end, an inward landscape glimpsed in passing in the course of about two minutes.

This is a section of Hector Berlioz' lyrical monodrama *Lélio ou le retour à la vie*. Intended as a sequel to the *Symphonie fantastique* and an awakening from the opium-induced dreams depicted there, with the main character imagining himself standing before his own tombstone. The section in question is entitled *Aeolian Harp – Recollections*, which hints at the formation of the music. The technical history of the Aeolian harp goes back to an invention by Athanasius Kircher in the mid-17th century. Twelve unison strings are stretched over a box with a sounding board and sound holes and is intended for outdoor use. The wind acting on the strings produces a variety of overtones, depending on the strength of the airstream and the thickness and tension of the strings. The tonal range can be anything up to six octaves. Needless to say, timbre and tone combinations are unaffected by human intervention, leaving aside technical aspects, but depend entirely on the movements of the air. The unexpected, the unforeseeable, is the norm, and not only the timbre but the actual process is unplanned, which stimulates the imagination. Chance prevails, with Berlioz an embodied absence of intent.

The Aeolian harp has always fascinated artists of various kinds, especially – non too surprisingly – composers, but also poets. Eduard Mörike's poem *Die Äolsharfe* has been set to music by both Brahms and Hugo Wolf, and in 1923 we find Henry Cowell composing a piano piece called *Aeolian Harp*. Further examples could be given, but more important for present purposes is the instrument's association with mythology. It is mentioned in Greek antiquity, from Homer onwards, with a description of Hermes inventing the lyre by letting the wind blow through the sinews of a tortoise shell. Startlingly similar is another version from the ancient world, attributing the invention, not of the lyre but of tone and with it the birth of music, to someone tripping over a tortoise shell with a tightened tendon, thereby producing a tone. In both instances the end product is random, unintentional. Jacques Handschin makes this myth the starting point of a polemic against previous theories concerning the origin of music. In his *Musikgeschichte* (pp. 29–30) he discusses Herbert Spencer's idea of music being derived from language, Charles Darwin's notion of a parallel between birdsong and music, with sexuality and reproduction as the driving force, and Karl Bücher's theory of music having originated as a means of rhythmically co-ordinating and facilitating shared physical labour. Handschin rebuts this last mentioned view by asking why, among "primitive" peoples, music is found to be associated with magic and religion more than with work. In more recent theories concerning the genesis of music, common activity or interactivity is held forth as a vital prerequisite, whether it takes place in the religious/magical sphere, forms part of a common rite or is articulated in play.

One thing which all these views have in common is that *the phenomenon* itself, the actual sounding, is conspicuous by its absence, is not regarded as the basic cause of the birth of music. Handschin opposes this view, and I quote:

"(...) this antique interpretation (...) has, by comparison with the above mentioned pseudo-scientific theories, a dual merit: 1. It begins with a precise concept of music by presupposing the musical tone (...) and in this way, unlike the scholars of our time, establishes, not just any characteristic whatsoever (*irgendein*) for music but the fundamental (*konstitutive*) characteristic. 2. It is related in a concrete way to man, or more exactly, man as being musical or receptive to music (...) who immediately proceeds to relate one tone to another according to inward and outward differences (pitch and key relation). In other words, if a mere animal had touched the tortoiseshell sinew, this would not have been music. It is also interesting that, according to the ancient view, the prototype of music is instrumental and not vocal."

What Handschin formulates here is a theory, not only concerning the origin of music but also concerning its essence, its ontology. Before we proceed to enlarge on this theme, both the view taken and the man taking it should be placed in a perspective of the history of ideas in philosophy, namely the philosophy of music.

Someone may possibly have gained the impression than in Handschin's case we are dealing with a theoretical musicology taken to extremes. He probably saw himself in this way, and *Der Toncharakter* carries the subheading *Eine Einführung in die Tonpsychologie*. But with his emphatic rejection of what he calls "pseudo-science" and his speculative approach based on the history of ideas, he qualifies for the philosophy division.

In the more general discussion of music, the terms "philosophy" and "aesthetic" are used interchangeably. *The New Grove's Dictionary of Music*. published in 1980, describes the subject field in an article headed "Aesthetics" running to 15 double-columned pages, whereas the 2001 edition renames the article "Philosophy of Music" and gives it twice as many pages. We may presume that during the interim the field has grown in importance, at the same time as there has been a shift of focus. Both aspects are connected: new ways of looking at things augment the sum total of knowledge as well as changing perspectives. Perhaps the most important thing to have happened in these twenty years is that the term "aesthetic" has been relativised to encompass the period from the mid-18th century onwards and has changed direction in favour of a more normative aspect: aesthetic is expected to answer the question of what is beautiful, while philosophy sets out to answer the question of what is true or probable. In addition, the term "aesthetic" is employed to characterise that which guides an artist's work, both in an overarching sense and in the individual case. Compositional deliberations are often classed as aesthetic, i. e. aesthetic becomes applied artistic practice, which in that case also applies to interpretation. With that kind of viewpoint, thinking *in* music becomes an aesthetic activity, while thinking *about* music becomes a philosophical one. Obviously it is the latter which concerns us here.

The term "philosophy of music" seems to presuppose a symbiosis or at least a close connection between music and philosophy. This very proximity, however, is questioned in the latest edition of *The New Grove's Dictionary*. The introduction to the article, subheaded "A sceptical beginning" and authored by Lydia Goehr, begins by noting that the Western discussion of philosophy is permeated by discussions both long and short, at the same time as similar philosophical discussions occur in the history of Western music. None of the known philosophers has devoted his thoughts exclusively to music, any more than known musicians have exclusively devoted themselves to philosophy – because then they would not have been musicians. On the other hand, nearly all big names in philosophy have at some time addressed music, just as eminent musicians have philosophised on their activity. Against this background, Goehr divides activities in the philosophy of music into three groups.

The first comprises philosophies expounding cosmological or metaphysical system in which music forms par of an explanation of the world. Names self-evident to us in this direction include the entire historical panorama Pythagoras via Boethius and Schopenhauer to Adorno. The second group contains philosophies dealing with different arts. Eduard Hanslick and large portions of Anglo-American philosophy are self-evident representatives of music. Last of all we have philosophies formulated by composers, musicians, theorists and critics – philosophies created, so to speak, from the inside, from professional experiences of music. Most often they are unsystematic and not aimed at presenting an explanation of the world. But occasionally they can employ a wider grasp, as is the case for example with Wagner, Stravinsky, Hindemith and Stockhausen.

The picture, then, according to Goehr, is not crystal-clear, and she points out that the philosophy of music mirrors the development of Western music in such a way that it is the most cherished genres on any particular occasion that determine which philosophical theory will prevail. She also raises the question of whether every field of knowledge, e. g. biology or law, can or should generate a philosophy specific to the discipline. Or music? She concedes that music, historically speaking, has had an extraordinary breadth and we need only consider its various utterances, such as production, interpretation, theory formation, reception, speech speculation, emotional expression and therapy to understand what she means.

Nevertheless, she takes the view that the connection between music and philosophy is too motley and manifold to be gathered together under the concept of "philosophy of music", and she therefore proposes the following formulation: "Philosophy and/or music may better capture their suggestive history of interactive equality and tension and leave dialectically open the issue of their relation".

So much for *The New Grove*. Now the question is: music and philosophy – how can one conceive of their mutual relationship? The relation being open, the field seems clear for various hypotheses and ideas. Let us begin with a generalisation concerning philosophy. Philosophy seems really to be concerned with two things: what we can know and how we should live. Music can enrich life, even if it cannot induce us to act in a way which is ethically and morally defensible. Music can also give us a deeper insight into the nature of the world, make us experience such elementary things as space and time emotionally. Perhaps indeed tone? Music as a fount of knowledge? Would philosophy perhaps benefit from being musicalised, being helped by music to understand itself better?

What questions are being addressed by the present-day philosophy of music? What do philosophers identify as philosophical problems relevant to music, what grabs them? To shed light on this, I have chosen two works by, respectively, Aaron Ridley and Stephen Davies, and I wish to make it clear from the start that my intention is not necessarily to take issue with their opinions but with the aid of their presentations to deepen my own. Both works significantly employ the term "Philosophy" as their main word. In addition they have the word "Theme(s)" in common, which suggests that they can be said with some degree of certainty to represent, to thematise, important tendencies. Ridley's theme is the conviction that music is a part of life, and so he is against all notions of "absolute" music, or, as he puts it, "music from Mars". Out of this theme he develops five variations, each exemplified by a work of music, and these variations in themselves can be said to constitute themes of the philosophy of music, namely: "Understanding", "Representation", "Expression", "Performance" and "Profundity". Davies for his part presents four themes: "Ontology", "Performance", "Expression" and "Appreciation", and we see at once the similarities between the two authors' thematisation. Music as expression and music as interpretation are one common denominator, another is the ontology of music, though Ridley for his part questions its significance. Both Ridley and Davies view music, so to speak, from above, eventually working their way down into its structures and implications so as to be able from these to uncover aspects of philosophical principle which in turn are expected to say something essential about the work. It is typical that both of them deal almost exclusively with Western music, though Davies points to Indonesian gamelan music as works without notation. In Lydia Goehr's grouping of music philosophers, these two authors, not very surprisingly, end up in group number two, along with Anglo-American philosophers and Eduard Hanslick.

Which group does Jacques Handschin belong to? There would seem to be no doubt that he belongs to Goehr's first group but at the same time is infinitely closer to Pythagoras than to Adorno. His philosophy is a philosophy of tones, and from their interaction there emerges a world of proportions. These manifest themselves in the well-known interval relations, in the relation between tone and number. What he says is that tones, and with it music, have certain basic properties which apply from one culture to another. He places the universals of music at the centre of attention and here Boethius's three basic concepts, reinterpreted by me, come into play. To Handschin the character of tone is encompassed by a universal of music, something bridging the gap between inward an outward. Here we see the philosophical-metaphysical side of Handschin's intellectual world: nothing in music stands for itself in isolation. Instead the precondition for the existence of the individual part is its inclusion in a wider context. Thus tones and music become an image of the Creation, in which man with his individual features forms part of a commonwealth of all living things. The world is harmonic and our endeavour should be to attain and portray that harmony.

Handschin's sounding world picture is very alluring, and so we should not throw ourselves unquestioningly into its embrace. His great merit, let it again be said, is that he puts *the phenomenon*, tone, the actually sounding, at the centre of attention. This happening in the form of myth makes the whole thing plain to see, communicates a Eureka experience. Let us think our way into the situation with the aid of imagination: early man, confronted by tones, is amazed. He has never experienced anything of the kind before; tone both frightens and enchants, the inexplicable is coupled with the urgently important. Tone *wants* something from us, but what? Are there other tones? We look for them and there prove to be many. Some sound perfectly well together, others more or less clash with each other and eventually one has a tone vocabulary which needs to be structured. And so begins the long march through the world's different music cultures, in which tone selection and the internal relations of tone differ greatly from one culture to another.

This compressed history of the world's music needs concretisation from both philosophy and music, and first in the field is a quotation from 'Schopenhauer's *Die Welt als Wille und Vorstellung*:

"I recognise in the deepest tones of harmony, in the bass, the lowest grades of objectification of will, unorganised nature, the mass of the planet. It is well known that all the high notes which are easily sounded and die away more quickly are to be regarded as a result of the deep base notes' partials. When the low notes are struck, the high notes too sound faintly, and it is a law of harmony that only those high notes may accompany the bass note which are already sounding along with it through its partials ... Bass, then, is for us in harmony with unorganised nature, the crudest mass, upon which all rests, and from which everything originates and develops, is in the world. Now, further, in the whole of the complemental parts which make up the harmony between the bass and the leading voice singing the melody, I recognise the whole gradation of the ideas in which the will objectifies itself. Those nearer to the bass are the lower of these grades, the still unorganised, but yet manifold phenomenal things; the higher represent to me the world of plants and beasts ... But to all these base and complemental parts which make up the harmony there is wanting that connected progress which belongs only to the high voice singing the melody .. while all these others have only a slower movement without a connection in each part for itself... In the *melody*, in the high, singing principal voice leading the whole and progressing with unrestrained freedom, in the unbroken significant connection of *one* thought from beginning to end representing a whole, I recognise the highest grade of the objectification of will, the intellectual life and effort of man." (Schopenhauer, p. 341–343)[1]

Schopenhauer shows in this passage that he knows what he is talking about on the subject of basic acoustic facts and fundamental compositional elements of his time, such as the relationship between melody and harmony. Even though he was not himself a practising musician, this is no amateur speaking. With his musical analogy he seeks to bring out the basic elements of his philosophy: the grouping of world-will-idea-representation is matched by the grouping of bass-harmony-melody, in which it is to be noted that the bass opens onto the abyss where nothing is audible any more.

Thus far the analogy presents little difficulty. But if we begin wondering what Schopenhauer's analogy could sound like if his philosophy, so to speak, were musicalised, associations with actually existing music appear, associations which he himself cannot possibly have had in mind. To me, his musical analogy makes a fairly perfect description of the overture to Wagner's *The Rhinegold* and with it the whole of *The Ring of the Nibelung*. With all desirable concretion: Schopenhauer's mention of "the deepest tones of harmony, in the bass," is matched in Wagner by a low, sustained tone which seems to lose itself in nothingness still deeper down

---

1   Translation (modified here) by R. B. Haldane and B. Kemp. Schopenhauer's italics.

and remains unchanged through all of the overture's 136 bars. Schopenhauer's wording, "the complemental parts which make up the harmony between the bass and the leading voice singing the melody" is matched in Wagner, first by the circling sound of the horns round each other in major triad tones, and later on by the broken triads of the strings and the scale movements of the woodwinds. Schopenhauer's "the high voice singing the melody, [which] alone moves quickly and lightly in modulations and runs" is matched by the entry of the Rhine-daughters, with their "Weia! Waga! Woge, du Welle". This musical process of two or three minutes duration is set in the River Rhine, where the sunlight eventually penetrates the deepest crannies. Just as in the Biblical book of *Genesis*, darkness hovers over the deep to begin with, but here the Creator's "Let there be light" is less dramatic.

The comparison with the Biblical creation story is more than casual. The overture to *The Rhinegold* has often and rightly been described as a Creation narrative in music, in which a world slowly takes shape, a world of giants, dwarves, gods, men, animated nature and, last but not least, by a new musical world of previously unheard sounds and motifs, with great capacity for characterisation and transformation. *Die Welt als Wille und Vorstellung*, in common with *The Ring of the Nibelung*, claims to be an explanation of the world, and Schopenhauer's musical analogy can be seen as an attempt to facilitate, for people with an interest in music, the understanding of his philosophy, as a kind of "Introduction". This pedagogical aspect is lacking in Wagner and thus distinguishes his overture from the philosopher's analogy, which in turn is bound up with the character of their respective cosmologies. Because of its medium, the word, Schopenhauer's is more a state, while Wagner's, thanks to tone and rhythm, is more to be likened to a process, a development.

Is there any other connection between the musical analogy and the overture, in addition to the aspects I have now broached? Can the two men's lives afford an opening, can there have been influence between them? Let us examine the facts available. Schopenhauer's work appeared in 1819, i. e. some 30 years before Wagner's description in *Mein Leben* of how and when the idea came to him in a semi-trance. The situation resembles that occurring when August Strindberg in *Stora Landsvägen*, his last completed drama, brings in a Japanese desirous of experiencing "the purifying, atoning power of fire" and asking the huntsman in the play to gather his ashes into the most previous of vases afterwards. The vase is to be inscribed with the Japanese man's name, and he has been named after his native city. That city is called Hiroshima, and Strindberg's text, once again, was written thirty-odd years before the event which has given the city a place in world history.

This latter association may seem a trifle too fanciful. Perhaps too there is something frightening about it: is such concrete prediction of the future really possible? Various values can be put on the Strindberg example. For my own part I have difficulty in shunning the glimpse of something, I know not what. Perhaps the somnambulatory assurance of an artist?

In Schopenhauer's case, though, we are treading on firmer ground, because there is a second party who could corroborate or deny the relevance of his musical analogy to the association I have asserted, namely Richard Wagner. Could he have been struck by Schopenhauer's analogy and had it in mind when drafting his overture to *The Rhinegold*? On closer chronological inspection, this proves to be out of the question. Schopenhauer's work was published in 1819 and only began to attract the attention of the public in the 1850s. Wagner drew the concluding line under his score in September 1854 and it was not until October that year that a friend tipped him off about *Die Welt als Wille und Vorstellung*. He read it over and over again a number of times between then and the following summer, and must therefore have been closely familiar with it. His collected writings include several highly appreciative remarks, of varying length, on Schopenhauer's work, including the music descriptions. He does not have a word to say concerning what seems to me the obvious parallelity, one also draws a blank in those entries in Cosima Wagner's diaries where Schopenhauer is mentioned.

Why is this? One reason may be Wagner's reluctance to speak about his own music. He often held forth about the ideas underlying his creativity, and he often scrutinises his characters in a bid to explain their characters and actions. He could also come up with apt characterisations of other music. Another reason may be his reluctance – understandable in itself – to acknowledge influences, as evidenced in his correspondence with Franz Liszt. But in this particular instance he could instead have been pleased at having Schopenhauer as his precursor and prophet. What a reaffirmation! But I think the explanation is to be sought in their personal relationship. True, they never actually met, but there was indirect contact between them. Wagner sent him the libretto – or, as he called it, "the poem" – of *The Ring of the Nibelung* with a deferential dedication, but never received any reply. On the other hand he heard, by devious paths, that Schopenhauer had spoken approvingly of what he had read – "he is a poet but no musician" – of which verdict Wagner remarked that it was at least better than the opposite. (C. Wagner I, 16 Jan. 1869). Perhaps he was disappointed over Schopenhauer not wishing to ascribe him the same significance as he had lavishly ascribed to Schopenhauer. With all respect to Schopenhauer's musical analogy, the fact remained that he, Wagner, was the music creator.

After this long digression – or, some might say, derailment – we will return to our starting point: the first human being's play with tone. In the overture we have been considering, Wagner represents the mythical situation as follows: the tone *e-flat* sounds, barely audibly, at the deepest imaginable pitch, and is joined by the tone of *b-flat* above the starting tone – a sounding fifth, in other words. After a while, curiosity impels him further and we hear rising fifths, fourths and major and minor thirds – in short, the *E-flat-major* triad or, if you will, the first six overtones. Savouring these tones, he lingers on them at the same time as the note values become progressively shorter, creating the illusion of a swifter tempo which does not really exist, given that the basic pulse remains unaltered. Eventually he admits major and minor seconds, thus completing the tone system, the major scale. Wagner behaves like man at the dawn of history and, moreover, tells us which intervals man chose, namely the most consonant ones. As we have already seen, these coincide with the ratio between integers according to the principle of: the simpler the ratio, the more consonant, mellifluous, the intervals. This choice has accompanied mankind through the millennia, and, not without reason, they are to be found in all known music cultures – the octave, the fifth and the fourth are constantly recurring key intervals in tone systems.

Wagner has already been invoked earlier in this essay as a species of King's evidence, namely in the reflections on his opening melody in *Parsifal*. Let us now call in another of the historical greats: Gottfried Wilhelm von Leibniz. Like most other philosophers, he has had something to say about music, which he calls "an unconscious exercise in arithmetic in which the mind does not know it is counting". What can he have meant by this? Handschin makes a suggestion, published in the anthology Ausgewählte Schriften under the heading *Über reine Harmonie und temperierte Tonleitern* (p. 297) and (in translation) reading as follows:

"(...) taken literally, this definition is easily ridiculed. But in a superior sense, all it tells us is that art is a beholding of proportions and that this is as true as the other proposition, namely that art is rooted in the emotional, in feelings. It is perhaps the different degrees of tension between these two elements which constitutes the essence of art, and the contemplation of these tensions is the basic problem addressed by theoretical musicology ."

Handschin has hit the nail on the head, especially if we substitute "philosophy of music" for "theoretical musicology". The myth-man-music constellation points the way to a philosophy of tones.

Tone and Space

In the beginning was space. Or, in the words of the Bible: "In the beginning God created the heaven and the earth. And the earth was without form, and void; and darkness was upon the face of the deep. And the Spirit of God moved upon the face of the waters." Which is to say: space came first, not time. According to the modern view, space and time are interdependent, but our usage seems to contradict this: chronological determinations such as "long" and "short" come from the vocabulary of space, we say "thereafter", not "then-after", we speak of "space of time". Space, to us, is more concrete than time, which justifies putting it at the centre of human experience. Given this starting point, it becomes natural to argue that geometry, the science of space, has, at least historically speaking, not been subordinated to chronometry, the science of time. In the classical notion of space and well into the 19th century, the concept of "space" can be regarded as a primary, elementary notion which, in everyday human life, has not been at all eroded by modern physical theories. These latter are the result of a process of abstraction occupying several centuries, whereas philology, archaeology and anthropology, on the other hand, show people in remote prehistory to have been incapable of peeling off a space concept from the spatial experience. In the dawn of human history, space was a casual array of concrete orientations, a diversity of local directions. This perception of space can have been co-ordinated with a concept of space common to a group, such as the family or tribe.

Not without reason, we have taken a religious document as our jumping-off point. The prophet Isaiah's vision of the seraphim calling to each other from great distances in praise of God comes in the same category. This religiously tinged perception of space is manifested in Judaism by the word for "place" (*makom*) becoming the name of the deity whose depiction was not permissible. Eventually the original meaning, "place", lapsed into oblivion and thoughts turned instead to God's omnipresence without any limitations of space. In Psalms 139:7-9, we read: "Whither shall I go from thy spirit? or whither shall I flee from thy presence? If I ascend up into heaven, thou art there; if I make my bed in hell. behold, thou art there. If I take the wings of the morning, and dwell in the uttermost parts of the sea; Even there shall thy hand lead me, and thy right hand shall hold me." In the Rabbinic scripture *Midrash Rabbah* we find the following statement: "He is the place of the world... We do not know whether G-d is the place of His world or whether His world is His place. But when the verse (Exodus 33:21) states, 'Behold, there is a place with Me,' it follows that G-d is the place of His world, but His world is not His place.". Much later, the philosopher Tommaso Campanella echoes this tradition with the statement: "The Lord is the dwelling of His world but His world is not His dwelling" (cit. *Rum, människa, musik*, p. 15). This equation of space and God is only possible in monotheist religions and, accordingly, not in the theology of ancient Greece. We find a musical instance of God's identity with space in the introduction to Arnold Schoenberg's opera *Moses and Aaron*, with Moses' invocation "Only one, infinite, thou omnipresent one, unperceived and inconceivable God!", a concentrated philosopho-religious pronouncement of the nature of being. In purely musical terms, this vision, reminiscent of Parmenides and the Eleans, is represented with the aid of the various possibilities of twelve-tone technique, where the audible result is an experience of symmetry, of a system both closed and wide open, symbolising God's infinity. The scene centres on God's revelation as a burning bush – or indeed as a guiding pillar of cloud and fire – which implies an identification of space with light. In the New Testament we read: "I am the light of the world" (Joh. 8:12), and this apotheosis of light becomes fundamental to late Neo-Platonism and medieval mysticism.

Religion, then, can be seen as an attempt to describe space. Philosophical reflection is another method, but before advancing that far we shall endeavour, with the aid of *Filosofilexikonet*, to test the possibility of systematising the meaning and use of the term "space". A distinction is made between mathematical space, i.e. geometric dimensions, physical space in which everything existing is present and movement occurs, and, finally, demonstrable space, which is experienced through the senses and is dominated by perspective and horizons. The interrelationship of these three forms of space is a much-discussed topic. Whereas mathematical space can have any number of dimensions, physical and demonstrable space is taken to be distinguished by three-dimensionality. In addition, the question arises whether these forms of space are Euclidian or non-Euclidian. According to more modern philosophy, the question of space being Euclidian or non-Euclidian is empirical, i.e. based on experience, which has not prevented a number of philosophers from claiming precedence for the Euclidian perception of dimension. The question of division of space is a further aspect. Are there space atoms, is space infinitely divisible, is it homogeneous or continuous? We recall Leibniz's dictum that "Nature makes no leaps" and Zeno's paradoxes, questioning the possibility of motion.

One can also problematise the concept of "vacuum", enquiring whether it is wholly or partly void or whether it must necessarily be filled. Newton maintained that space was a species of container for matter, which is to say that space and matter are separate entities. This gives us Newton's "absolute space", the alternative to which is Leibniz's interpretation of space as relations between objects. In modern times, Einstein propounds the theory of relativity, abolishing the notion of an absolute space. Last of all, does space exist as an independent phenomenon? Is it not in fact a way of perceiving reality, in Kantian terminology a form of intuition?

Thus far *Filosofilexikonet*. A number of reflections spring to mind. The systematisation of different perceptions of space is fundamentally based on a long historical development condensed in the form of a dictionary article – understandably enough. But the various historical views do not disappear but lead a life of their own. Philosophy shares this characteristic with art: it does not "overcome" the generation immediately preceding, but nuances and contradicts it. The old lives on, side by side with the new, and can sometimes put forth new shoots which lead a much later philosophy into new paths, causing it to take a Eureka view of its precursors. Leibniz's logical enquiries, for example, have been echoed and taken on a new lease of life in the work done by Bertrand Russell in the same field, and the Pythagoreans' ideas of the harmony of the spheres, of the universe as one big sound box, can be said to crop up in the now so topical string theory, which seeks to unite quantum mechanics with the theory of relativity and thereby to present a uniform physical world description. The word "physical" is carefully chosen; no mention is made there of "harmony", nor of tone and music. But a philosophical interpretation of string theory could very well lead to a vision of the world as one colossal symphony, a notion which Gustav Mahler had in mind in his eighth symphony, *Die Sinfonie der Tausend*, and which is reiterated in the well-known rejoinder to Jean Sibelius: "The symphony must be like the world: it must embrace everything."

Somewhat drastically speaking, philosophy is equivalent to the history of philosophy, and the same goes for the philosophy of space and perception of space. Without going too deeply into detail, it should thus be able, with the assistance of works by Max Jammer and Otto Friedrich Bollnow listed in the bibliography, to paint a panorama of space as idea and representation, thereby deepening our perception of space beyond the religious aspects which have already been dealt with.

At first the scene is dominated by Aristotle, whose authority went unchallenged for centuries. He thinks of space as a series of receptacles or spheres inside each other, ranging all the way from the man-ship-river-riverbed relationship to the planetary spheres emanating from the earth. Underlying the view thus hinted at is the question of whether motion requires repose. Aristotle's, and thus the ancient world's, answer is largely in the affirmative, underlying Zeno's famous paradoxes of the impossibility of motion. Space is perceived as static, and there is no such thing as empty space.

Despite Aristotle's authority, there is all the time an intra-ancient opposition which also gains adherents among later Arab philosophers, asserting the possibility of a relation between space and motion, perhaps indeed one of interdependence. With the Copernican revolution, well into the Christian era, the Aristotelian view of space can be said to have come to the end of the road: the notion of the world as a sequence of spheres packed inside each other and the concomitant, coherent definition of both place and space with the earth at the centre gives way to an array of heavenly bodies hovering freely in the vacuum, outer space, and with the sun as their unifying central point. Space becomes infinite.

Now Isaac Newton enters the scene, quickly attaining an authority comparable to Aristotle's. He distinguishes between absolute and relative space, of which the former, "in its own nature, without regard to anything external, remains always similar and immovable." The latter, by contrast, "is some movable dimension or measure of the absolute spaces; which our senses determine by its position to bodies". This Newtonian dual concept of space clashes with Leibniz, to whom space is merely a system of relations having neither metaphysical nor ontological existence, which means to say that space is an order of simultaneously existing data, a combination of space and time where time comes first, as many later philosophers have also asserted. Newton's inability to accept Leibniz's view is connected with a religious dimension which increasingly merges with and motivates his scientific activity. Judaic cabbalism and Neo-Platonism play a role in his identification of absolute space with God. Scientific enquiry, to Newton, is not at the centre of things but is valued instrumentally, as a means to a superior end. Absolute space, according to Newton, is God's antenna, which does not preclude Newton having been guided to his conclusions about the "absolute" by an ideal of perfection. It should be added that the notion of absolute space and absolute time – and why not absolute music? – has always exerted a powerful attraction on human sensibility. Clarity and strictness, wisdom and conclusiveness appear to be guaranteed.

Newton's authority lasted for some 200 years, until Albert Einstein's presentation of the theory of relativity. The idea of absolute space was now relegated from living scientific debate to the department of the history of ideas, but with full military honours, not least from Einstein himself: " Newton, forgive me. You found the only way which, in your age, was just about possible for a man of highest thought and creative power. The concepts which you created are, even today, still guiding our thinking in physics, although we now know that they will have to be replaced by others farther removed from the sphere of immediate experience, if we aim at a profounder understanding of relationships" (*Concepts of Space*, p. 173). The "other concepts" apostrophised by Einstein can be termed a development of Newton's relative space – that is, quite simply, the theory of relativity, the kernel of which is that the beholder's physical position decides his judgement of both space and motion and, with them, time.

Other spatial concepts have also been called into question, in particular three-dimensionality, whose first great name is Euclid. In modern scientific thought, the three-dimensionality of space or the four-dimensionality of space-time is seen as a coincidence, justified only by experience. When non-Euclidean geometry makes its first appearance, when space can be considered multidimensional, classical three-dimensionality becomes a problem, at the same time as, paradoxically enough, this has led to a growth of interest in finding arguments for it. Efforts are being concentrated, not least, on clarifying the very concept of "dimension", which at present seems to imply the use of various "subspaces" combined with the inductive character of the definition. By this last mentioned is meant a conclusion in which "the premises support the conclusion without logically entailing it" (*Filosofilexikonet*).

The expression "empty space" is another moot point. Since any attempt at experimentally "proving" its existence would disrupt its very character of empty space, the simplest way of responding to the intellectual imperative of imparting some kind of meaning to the alleged emptiness of space may be to say that space is empty if *no instrument gives a reading when introduced into it* (*Concepts of Space*, p. 190).

A word or two should also be said concerning the influence of modern particle physics on notions of space and time. Particle physics queries the notion of space and time being the basic constituents of physical thinking, which leads to the thought of the traditional space and time concepts as being applicable only in large contexts, macro systems. This in turn has prompted scientists to suggest that these concepts arise out of, but lack analogies in, the properties of microscopic particles. Another opening is the attempts now being made to unite quantum physics with general relativity theory into a single, unitary theory, e.g. string theory. This raises the question of the number of dimensions in space.

Max Jammer concludes his presentation with the following lament: "Perhaps it is true that the hope that physical research can resolve the physical problems is just as vain as the hope that philosophical thought can resolve the physical problems of space" (*Concepts of Space*, p. 251). The word "problems" can be given a broader allusion insofar as the whole of philosophy as such can be regarded as a problematisation of the ostensibly given and self-evident. As mentioned earlier, moreover, philosophy problematises itself in that ideas which are "vanquished" appear to have a knack of cropping up again and never really being properly vanquished.

In what way could the spatial philosophies presented here be of consequence for music? Or for art of any kind? Some artists have drawn inspiration from scientific theories and modes of thinking. This can be instanced with Salvador Dali and Yannis Xenakis, the latter being both composer and architect. In his stochastic music he employs musical structures based on the probability calculations of logic, which, however, is devoid of spatial aspects, unlike the discussion occurring in some of my own works, more exactly, a discussion of the importance of the octave for our perception of musical space. There I distinguish between octave-based and non-octave-based tone systems, the sole representative of the latter being the atonality of Arnold Schoenberg. This latter could be analogous to multi-dimensional space, while the former corresponds to the three-dimensionality of space. Just as three-dimensionality is a special case of multi-dimensionality, is included in it, so octave-based space could be a special case of the atonal, be included in it. In a word: Einstein *v.* Newton, Schoenberg *v.* Pythagoras – and all the others.

* * *

So far we have been treating space partly as an aspect of religious contemplation and partly in the form of theories about mathematical-physical space. But there is also another kind of space, that which we experience daily through our senses, which we adapt to and within which we live out our lives. We call this experienced space. The boundaries between these different spaces need not always be hard and fast, because they can borrow features from each other, conceptualisation and concrete experience can be akin to each other. Nevertheless there is a fundamental difference which can be formulated as follows: mathematical-physical space, that which incarnates idea and conception, has no central point, is uniform, homogeneous, has no qualitative differences between different points/locations, is of infinite extent in all directions. Experienced space, by contrast, space as experience, has a centre determined by the experiencing individual's position in the space where his *upright walk* is the determinant. Places/locations are qualitatively different and man divides space according to content. The boundaries between the different contacts are both fluid and sharply defined. Experienced space is unstable and at first finite, both inhibiting and furthering human life, suggesting a symbiosis of man and space. Space then becomes more than a Kantian form of presentation and rather a general form of man's relation to life. It is a means of self-realisation to the ego, threatening or protecting, it is a passage or refuge, it is distance or at home, it is man's own organ or his opponent. Space here is not neutral but, on the contrary, full of meanings, not only expressions of a subjective feeling but also properties of the space itself. Space is a correlate to man and one man's space is different from any other man's. It is also possible to create in one's imagination a space which has been dubbed "the poetic of space". Space as expressions of a poet's powers of imagination? Or why not those of a musician/composer?

Space, then, is man's form of life. Man's upright gait causes him to be integrated with a system of axes, horizontal and vertical, from which three lines of direction crystallise out: up-down, forwards-backwards, right-left (sideways). These directions differ in meaning and significance. Up-down is, so to speak, in the nature of things, indicative as it is of man's position twixt heaven and earth. It is man's inevitable predicament, meaning that experience of height and depth is elementary, existential, the very precondition of human life. The forwards-backwards direction, on the other hand, adds a dynamic element to man's spatial experience: he is heading somewhere, he travels, migrates. He can turn through 180 degrees and in doing so reverse these two opposites. He is also heading somewhere in a metaphorical sense, for the completion of a task and then returning, either with his mission accomplished or else having failed to accomplish it. Return, then, can mean coming to one's senses, reflecting. The sideways dimension, finally, has, as mentioned previously, two directions: right and left. These are basically equivalent, even though religion and perhaps convention give priority to the right side.

We see how space and man's movement within it are immediately charged with meanings which go far beyond the notional structure of space. A space with no meaning does not seem to exist. Let me give a few examples, beginning with the centre of space. Man's immediate experience tells him that the central point should be at the centre of observation, i. e. the bridge of the nose, but we have to consider man's complex relation to space: he moves "in" this stationary space while at the same time having a subjective system of reference to it. The central point can be "home" or the object of homesickness. In days gone by the centre was one's own community or country, cf. the Middle Kingdom. After the great discoveries and the globalisation which followed them, the "centre" concept came to be problematised, as can be seen on maps of the world, with Europe losing its central position to the Pacific. "Centre" can also be when people in former ages emigrate, taking with them the post of the seat of honour to the new country, as the saga tells us happened with the foundation of Reykjavik. A further aspect is the finiteness of the world, and for certain "primitive" peoples the world ends beyond the area under their control.

Horizon and perspective are two other aspects of man's spatial experience. The horizon has two characteristics. Firstly, it limits our field of vision in all directions, at the same time as we never reach the horizon, because it is forever retreating, and secondly, it imposes no limits at all but affords wide prospects for a movement forward, all the time beckoning us further. The horizon can only exist in symbiosis with man: he is the horizon's *sine qua non*. The horizon – that which units heaven and earth, the blue vault with the green, grey or red earth – makes it possible for man to feel at home and safe.

Perspective for its part enables us to see things from a particular angle or in a particular direction. Things grow smaller if distance increases, and viewed from the air they look different. Things in the foreground conceal those in the background. Through perspective, things are ordered according to nearness and distance in relation to man in the centre of his space. Thus horizon and perspective belong together. Perspectives arrange things within the horizon, while the latter imparts stability to the former. These terms can also be used metaphorically, as in "spiritual horizon", "new perspective" and so on.

So far we have dwelt on illuminated space, whether basking in daylight or in artificial lighting, but there are of course a number of different lighting conditions by which clarity is obscured: dusk, dawn, mist, falling snow etc. In a combination of mist and dusk, for example, space can sometimes assume menacing forms, an experience portrayed in Goethe's and Schubert's *Erlkönig*. In the twilight world, man feels exposed and the object of a thousand unknown observers. On the other hand, dusk can also be warm and intimate, and that is a world where sleep is close at hand.

From day via dusk we come to the night. Progress through nocturnal space is guided by other senses than just vision, and above all by hearing and touch. One can imagine walking along a road at night in special lighting conditions, hearing distant sounds etc. Or groping one's way through a space, especially if it is an unfamiliar one. Nocturnal space contains more than light, it does not stretch/extend itself like the illuminated space but touches us more immediately, enclosing and penetrating us. We are permeable to darkness, we merge with space. Another characteristic of nocturnal space is that, unlike the clear, sober spaces of daytime, it is opaque and secretive. We stand there face to face with the unknown. There is no distance there, no real extent, but even so a peculiar depth which differs from the depth dimension of daytime, with its height and breadth. Depth is night's only dimension. In addition one can associate with pre-logical forms of thought, activate the nocturnal mystique of Romanticism as it appears in Novalis and in Wagner's *Tristan and Isolde*. Personal identity tends to be suspended, as does the difference between subject and object, something which affects animist trains of thought such as belief in superstition and ghosts. One might speak of an original spatiality corresponding to the subject's original state, from which subsequent modification of the spatial concept have evolved.

Space, then, seems to be a place of sense and will, dependent on man's state of mind. But it is also a place for the identification of objects and for purposive action. A pivotal role is played here by man's dwelling, his way of building a home, various room functions and the meaning of doors, thresholds, windows etc. But now I would like to concentrate on this matter of motion in space, where the degree of purposiveness eventually thins out and turns into something else.

Movement requires roads and, in more recent times, railways and, eventually, air routes. In order to utilise these possibilities, one needs an errand, at least to begin with. One travels on business, visits relations, attends a conference or goes away on holiday. Together with these purposive movements, there occurs another phenomenon, namely the spatial experience which the journey itself gives rise to. Imagine a car trip. The forward surge one experiences on a car journey also affects the character and dimensions of space. In the car there is only one meaningful direction – forwards. Sideways is unthinkable, backwards a contradiction in terms, because the direction then switches over to forwards. The road is nothing one stops on, except for a break. It becomes the future and man is subordinated to the flow of traffic, merges with it. All one's attention is concentrated on the narrow strip of road, with its perils and possibilities, at least if one is sitting behind the wheel. Things beside one are reduced to stage flats in the corner of one's eye, are not a space in the true sense, are as unattainable in the speed situation as the moon once used to be. The driver is no longer moving in the landscape but instead is passing by it. The purpose of this motion tends to slither into a spatial experience in itself, with the thrill of speed as a prominent element and with the relation between near and far also playing a role.

Walking is one kind of spatial movement that nowadays lacks a clear purpose. At the beginning of Schubert's *Die schöne Müllerin*, the miller sings "*Das Wandern ist des Müllers Lust, das Wandern*". We may add that this applies, not only to millers but to many other people who derive a very special kind of pleasure from activities like strolling, hiking and cycling – moving slowly through the landscape and savouring its colours, sounds and fragrances, an essentially different experience from motoring. A person moving on foot has a different relation to the road from the motorist's. For very obvious reasons, he avoids busy roads and instead resorts to paths which lead him deep into the landscape, the space. He walks for the sake of it, though this does not prevent him from having a destination, e. g. a viewing point or a pub. The absence of intent makes urgency an unknown concept. The walker is often absorbed in himself, the stuff that dreams are made of.

This very absence of intent leads us on to another kind of motion in space: dancing. Movement with a purpose or destination is essentially different from the motion of the dance. Here we have to do with two forms of movement. The movements of the dance are incomprehensible in relation to principles of feeder routes, road networks. Walking backwards we experience as a constraint, dancing backwards as a spontaneous act. In the ultimate analysis, this is due to the optical, everyday space having a direction, above all as regards the forward movement of walking. Retreat in this connection is a deplorable form of behaviour, contrary to the fundamental impulse of optical space. Dancing, on the other hand, is impervious to this aspect because it has no reference to direction at all. The everyday space has a central point: we leave home and return home. Dancing has no such sense of going away and coming back – any direction or place is as good as any other. Walking, we measure space, we pace it, so to speak, whereas the motion of dancing has no natural end and could go on indefinitely, no matter how small the room and how long the time. Dancing moves in a homogeneous space with no directions and, what is more, it creates a space of its own. It borders on music.

* * *

Both *Concepts of Space* and *Mensch und Raum* give us a number of concepts and terms which we would have little difficulty in applying to music. Height and depth, direction and place, density and sparseness, mass and extent – all these concepts and more besides are cases in point. All of them come from mathematical-physical space, but the flora of terms has to be supplemented from experienced space: light and shade/darkness, near and far, shape and colour, wealthy and emptiness/desolation. To this is added the transition between them, with motion and space reinforcing one another.

These very two phenomena, motion and space, are of the utmost interest for present purposes. Both mathematical-physical and experienced space are connected with motion, as is made abundantly clear by both Max Jammer and Otto Friedrich Bollnow. The fact is that space will allow itself to be identified and described solely with the aid of motion, through which it acquires form and content. Music is generally regarded as a phenomenon which shapes and represents time through movement and change. But if these two phenomena, and so time with them, are intimately bound up with space in a kind of symbiosis – i. e. the space-time of the theory of relativity – would it not be possible to see music as primarily a spatial phenomenon? This, at least, is the view I have outlined in the opening chapter of *Pythagoras' Sträng*, suggesting a rewording of Eduard Hanslick's famous definition of music, my version of which runs: "Tönend bewegter von Ausdruck getragener Raum" – "sounding and mobile space borne up by expression". Splitting this definition into its constituent parts, the words "sounding" and "expression" are most immediately referable to experienced space, while "mobile" and "space" belong essentially to mathematical-physical space. But the situation is more complex than that: both "mobile" and "space" can also be applied to experienced space, while "sounding" implies the numerical relations between the tones, i. e. looks towards mathematical-physical space. This does not mean that we must necessarily believe in the harmony of the spheres, it is just another way of saying that music is Janus-faced, is both nature and nurture.

We have now finally reached the point where tone, and with it music, can be placed at the centre of things. Background and preconditions have been created, the framework is in position. The question now is how man experiences and fashions tone and music on the basis of his perception of space and his notions of it.

* * *

Let us now, with the aid of imagination, put ourselves in a situation where we are confronted by tones. From nothingness a melody is suddenly heard, sustained by human voices. It rises and falls, pauses on a repeated tone, launches into lengthy convolutions of tone. We admire the nicely balanced alternation between steps and leaps, we distinguish certain central tones which are wound about and ornamented, we sense a word and a text which are shot through with light and, through the tones, attain a gentle ecstasy. Absorption and intensity are the key words for this way of making music.

This kind of music is dependent on being played in a limited space with qualities which both guide the performance and at the same time highlight the qualities of the music. The relation between space and music is symbiotic: the music comes from nowhere, is suddenly just there, insinuating itself and almost caressing the space, reaching into its furthest corners. The room for its part envelops the music, reinforcing it and at the same time softening any sharp edges it may have. Direction and development are wholly absent, all we have is a mobile state circling round itself.

But a space can be constructed in such a way as to permit or indeed inspire music with a clear direction, music in which the location of the sound source plays an important structural role. St Mark's, Venice, is a famous example of this kind, with its opposing choir lofts, where in about 1600 the effects were tested of vocal and instrumental ensembles, as it were, duelling with each other, answering and echoing each other. This "Venetian polychoralism" made a very important difference to the ensuing development of 17th century music, whether in churches, theatres or elsewhere, and compositionally it was manifested by the alternation of emergent instrumental music between soloists and orchestra and in what is termed terrace dynamics, i. e. abrupt, sometimes echo-like contrasts between *forte* and *piano*.

Another ecclesiastical space of interest is Les Invalides in Paris, which has four narrower spaces emanating from a central one, making the total space cruciform. This inspired Hector Berlioz, in his *Requiem* (1837) and the *Dies irae* movement of it depicting the Last Judgement, to position a brass ensemble in each of the four spaces to illustrate the dramatic and terrifying situation and its inevitability, its horrors converging from all directions. Characteristically enough, this arrangement does not occur in any other part of the composition and is therefore to be seen as an exception confirming the rule, namely that the spatial distribution of sound sources at this point in time was not, generally speaking, at the centre of composers' attention.

During the 20th century the situation changes again, not least as a result of advances in sound technology, which made sound sources easily separable and important parts of the compositional idea. Already in the 1950s we find Karlheinz Stockhausen writing his *Gruppen für drei Orchester,* and for the 1970 World Exposition in Osaka he had a spherical concert hall built in which specially composed music comes from every direction – from above, from below and from the side. Without having had the opportunity of hearing the result on the spot, I can imagine that, with every direction as good as any other, the sense of direction vanishes. Total direction becomes a total absence of direction and we find ourselves in a situation resembling the listener's situation in the experience we have just been imagining of melody hovering in space. We are enclosed in a round of sound which in turn is embraced by a material space and perhaps a religious or meditative feeling comes over us – none too surprisingly in view of Stockhausen's spiritual development.

We have touched on the term "concert hall". The reality it covers is a social development beginning in the first half of the 18th century. I refer to the emergence of the middle class, the economic and cultural aspirations distinguishing that social class, and its agenda-setting ambitions. The public concert becomes the most important weapon of music culture for asserting its individuality. This is an event taking place within a space defined by walls and ceiling and which, to begin with, was decided more by chance and availability. It is only in more recent centuries that events of this kind have tended more and more to take place on premises constructed for the purpose, giving us the concept of "concert hall acoustics".

What are the hallmarks of good acoustics for musical purposes? Answers vary, depending on the music performed, both the degree of amalgamation capacity *and* individualisation being important criteria. Generally speaking, what we have to primarily consider is the music which brought forth the phenomenon of the concert hall and the mentality in which that music was rooted. Western music can be thought of as an ongoing process of rationalisation in which tonal system, instrument tuning and rhythmic structure are simplified more and more, not to say streamlined. In the music which emerges during the 18th century, the emphasis is on harmony, balance, organised interaction. As a result, instead of instrumental ensembles with a heterogeneous timbre, a homogeneous timbre ideal increasingly asserts itself, and a collection of instruments is replaced by *one* instrument – the orchestra. This body of sound develops a structure which, certain attempted breakouts notwithstanding, holds good today in all essential respects: woodwinds, brass, strings and a percussion section. The string instruments are the backbone, tasked with holding the orchestral sound together and smooth down certain rough edges. The room in which the music is played serves as a "sound mixing box" (Wiggen, p. 14). The listener situation is such that a number of people have gathered with the shared intention of participating in music, allowing themselves for a while to be socially integrated and at the same time to be included in and become part of a wider unit, namely the sound mixing box whose composition and distribution ensures the harmony aimed for. The fact of the music coming from in front *towards* the listener is of secondary importance; the experience of direction *in* the room does not really signify. The fact of music in itself often communicating powerful experiences of direction is another story, connected with music's own spatial character.

The concert hall situation can be said to have been the norm for modern man's experience of music in space, as becomes apparent when it spills over into other spaces. The church, for example, has more and more been enlisted for concert activities having no connection with acts of worship, and in church we listen as if we were in the concert hall and we "listen past" those properties of the room which are not adapted to such activities. But above all it is the private, individual room that has been invaded by the concert hall with the aid of modern technology – the gramophone record, the recoded tape, loudspeakers. At home or in the seminar room we build our own concert hall, and our experience is equivalent to that which a "proper" concert hall can offer – but at the same time different. The listener situation of the great concourse is replaced by the situation of the small circle or the individual person, a situation where one can imagine or enter into the great concourse and see the orchestra or musicians before one in full swing. Music in the home, if you will.

The expression "music in the home" has, of course, another, older meaning: that of sitting at one's instrument, alone or in the company of others, and making music, with or without listeners, for the sheer joy of it and to the best of one's ability. Many musician portraits from earlier periods of history show a few people playing and singing together in a room of a more intimate character. The music is adapted to the size and volume of the room, the instruments used are both softer and sharper, as for example with the gamba, a stringed instrument of introvert, intimate character. This is really a matter of music primarily for performers, for which an audience of outsiders is not a necessary precondition. People in the 17th century were very much aware of each room demanding its own particular music, and a flora of terminology evolved for distinguishing between music's different functions.

We have been discussing music in a space delimited by walls and a ceiling and with various functions and, not least, characters. Whether it is music that creates the space or the space that creates the music is a chicken-and-egg sort of question. We will content ourselves with noting that space and music influence each other, that the seclusion of the room acquires life and movement through the music. But what happens to the music in a room where walls and ceiling have disappeared, where the boundary becomes the horizon and where other sounds also come into play? We must consider music in *the open air – free space* – open to wind and weather.

When seclusion within the four walls of the room no longer prevails, the *ipso facto* central position of music also ceases to exist. The concentrated listener is transformed into a more casual one, and the performers have to take up the struggle against what, in the closed room, would be considered disturbances. All of us have at one time or another come up against music outdoors, and an umbrella term for this phenomenon might perhaps be "promenade concerts", which inevitably arouses certain associations. But, disregarding those associations, it is perfectly possible to generalise the name as denoting music outdoors, whether the music or the audience or both are in motion. In the first instance one can imagine listeners passing by a stationary band in a town park or a classic spa where they submit to a regimen of taking the waters. Or why not buskers, to whom one throws a coin? In the second instance the first thing that springs to mind is the changing of the guard – soldiers marching up, say, to a royal palace, between spectators lining the route – native and foreign tourists, plus locals who happen to be passing by. The third possibility, that of both audience and music being in motion or capable of moving, is found in outdoor concerts, the space for which is marked by groups of loudspeakers from which electronically generated, tape-recorded music flows forth. The sounds migrate between the loudspeakers, the space is not delimitated but mobile, and through this mobile space people stroll, by both accident and design.

All these examples have one thing in common: music in free space is surrounded by other events which are not related to it. From this, two conclusions can be drawn. One of them has to do with the way in which, despite the lack of coherence, we are to understand music and its surroundings. Imagine the changing-of-the-guard situation: if we linger in the place where we happen to be, we hear the music coming nearer and nearer up till the moment when the band is right in front of us, after which the music moves away and eventually becomes inaudible. In addition we hear the footfalls of the marching bandsmen/soldiers, which we have no difficulty in integrating with the music. But all the time we hear something else as well: other bystanders' remarks, traffic noise, the shrieking of gulls, perhaps a steam whistle. As we already know, sounds of this kind are termed "concrete" or "acousmatic". The everyday acoustic world surrounds the music and possibly some of us permit the ear to integrate the music with the acousmatic world, permit the music to become just another sound. All the same, I think that most of us would automatically keep these two worlds of sound apart and, at most, find their interrelationship not lacking a comic element.

The second conclusion one can draw from the situation of music outdoors is that we are in fact dealing with two spaces. Back to the changing of the guard. The acousmatic space is stationary, and the music moves through it like a body or an object moving within the enveloping world of everyday sounds. This body has density and sparseness and could thus be said to have a mass of variable nature. It fills a certain amount of time counted in minutes and seconds and thus has an extent. But at the same time it forms within itself a relational network with various parts, causing it to resemble a space traversed by connections. Here music assumes a spatial character which transcends the fact of its being located in a space.

We are dealing, then, with various spaces within which music sounds and where both phenomena form part of an interplay. Doubtless further examples could be adduced of spaces with music specially adapted to them, a kind of functional fragmentation. But instead a space will be touched on here which lacks the functional implications characterising spaces created by man: *the vacuum*. Music in a vacuum – what is that? In the first instance perhaps one thinks of Pythagoras's vision of the harmony of the spheres and its recurrence in the string theory of our own time, insofar as such a parallel can be drawn. Then one's thoughts turn to the Swedish composer Karl-Birger Blomdahl's "space opera" *Aniara*, which begins and ends with music intended to represent outer space, empty and black. On closer reflection, though, we realise that the music is being played in an opera house with a stage, orchestra pit and auditorium, and that it *depicts* the vacuum, without being present in it. The depiction is very suggestive, but it takes as its starting point the inherent spatiality of the music – which is something different and something more.

* * *

First a self-quotation: "Melody also presents another spatial aspect which does not only or even mainly have to do with the space within which it sounds. Music seems to move in the celestial heights and at the same time the abysmal depths, describing both its own space and the space around it, creating an aura of space around itself. Just as the bumble bee ought not really to be capable of flying, so melody seems to defy the laws of nature, neither plunging into the abyss nor vanishing into the ether. Its own cramped space and limited movements are the precondition for its hovering, like a narrow, golden ribbon, between the extremes of existence, between height and depth. Since melody circles round itself, time itself seems to have come to a standstill, ceased to exist" (*Pythagoras' Sträng*, p. 95).

But space has not! As the above passage maintains, music has a space of its own with height and depth and with connections between the two. Even if time has stood still, motion has not, and this is a precondition for our being able to apprehend space at all. It is a transparent space of movement and life, reflecting a sense of life and an explanation of the world, that of the Christian faith.

Out of this space, however, there emerges another space, Gregorian plainsong is given counter-voices and transformed out of recognition. Musical space becomes compact, is broadened and acquires kinetic energy. The tool used is written codification, notation. The historical process can be summed up as follows.

Compact space is manifested in such a way that the Gregorian melody pauses on long, sustained tones round which, at most, three more voices are established. All of them stay close to the sustained tone, with a combined range seldom exceeding an octave, which justifies the characterisation of the space as compact, not to say solid. The effect is underlined by the surrounding parts all the time crossing each other, changing places, conveying the impression of teeming life within a narrow frame. The surrounding parts are rhythmically distinguished by dance-like movements contrasting sharply with the sustained tones and endowing the teeming space with a powerfully forward-propelling kinetic energy.

This is what Western music can have sounded like in about 1200 in the circle round Notre Dame in Paris. During the centuries that followed, this musical space was developed to a point where both higher and lower registers were incorporated, until by about 1600 the aggregate space of music comprised some three octaves. Of particular interest is the conquest of the lower sound areas which results in the Baroque emphasis on what was called continuo ("thoroughbass"), i. e. music's foundation. This, in a manner of speaking, had a precursor in the long, sustained melody which was eventually transformed and integrated with the composition as *cantus firmus* – firm song. The term sounds almost like *terra firma* – firm ground – and perhaps music at the beginning of the 17th century can be said to have acquired firm ground under its feet, to have touched down. This in turn means that the musical space had been concretised: the almost virtual space of Gregorian melodies, where, aided by imagination, we listen into a space, height and depth with no gravity, is superseded by a space with concrete height and depth, with density and sparseness and with extent. These properties are underlined by the visual impressions conveyed by the notation: we read it from the top downwards or vice versa, and from left to right. Height and depth are made visible by the positioning of the different registers, from the very highest, the descant, through the intermediate registers to the very lowest, the bass. The course of the music, its extent, can be followed, not only with the ear but the eye as well. Links between different stages, densification and dilution, the mobile character of the music, are phenomena also evident from the notation, which sometimes conveys the impression of a solid, irresistible onward surge. The space of music is a movable space with both upward and downward and forward directions.

However seductive the terms height and depth, forwards and backwards and, not least, movement, may be, we must be able to problematise them to make them applicable to music. Western linguistic usage is not uniform and the French for "high", for example, is *aigu*, meaning "sharp" or "pointed". This could suggest that the possibility of discerning differences of pitch is not so much spatial as a quality of timbre. In the ancient world the terms "high" and "low" were inverted, which presumably had to do with the way in which the *kithara* was held, the higher or sharper-sounding tones being produced at the bottom of the fingerboard, while the lower or softer sounding ones landed, technically speaking, further up. It is almost too much of a coincidence that, when Western polyphony began to be noted down, the highest, "sharpest" voices were put at the top of the page, which seems to suggest that height and depth were genuinely experienced. This is corroborated by the highest voice being designated *superius*, "highest", while the lowest was called *bassus*, "low". But there is also the possibility of the arrangement of notation having "beguiled" us into hearing height and depth in music, which, if it is the case, would further reinforce our two-dimensional hearing – our hearing both horizontally and vertically – and that we have here an example of the power of writing over thought. Even if this were the case, it would not, to my mind, detract from the mentality-related strength of this two-dimensional hearing, which, accordingly, it would seem fair to consider fundamental.

Turning now from aspects of mental history to a more systematic approach, we are faced with an interesting problem. We experience music as spatial and at the same time as something in motion. But does music move and are tones higher or lower in a physical-acoustic sense? On closer inspection this is not the case. Tones do not move, other than in the sense of sound waves moving through the air and evoking an experience of tone. This is neither high up nor deep down nor anywhere between the two, it is everywhere and nowhere. Why, then, do we persist in speaking of motion and space in music? One possible explanation, launched by Roger Scruton, is that we are dealing here with a metaphorical way of thinking whereby we transfer the experience of motion and space in the world around us to tones and thus to music (*The Aesthetics of Music*, p. 91–92).

In *Pythagoras' Sträng* I attempted, using examples from a number of symphonic movements by Bruckner and Sibelius, to exemplify a spatial approach. Re-reading it, I am struck by two things: firstly, the description is peppered with terms for different kinds of lighting, with words like "brilliant" and "beam of light" playing a pivotal role. Secondly, progress from one space to another is asserted, with a door being said either to slide open or have its lock picked, and where the contrast between confinement and opening is characteristic. Space is dramatised and the spatial concept coming closest is that distinguishing certain aspects of Bollnow's *Mensch und Raum*. But these examples are perhaps special pleading, as would be the case if I were only to adduce sections of other music with great simultaneous distance between height and depth, successive contrasts between different registers and so on. From the mass of existing repertoire it would be hard to distil a serviceable method of analysis for spatiality as a thoroughgoing feature of music while continuing to restrict ourselves to current spatial concepts, i. e. the mathematical-physical and experienced space. These can help to shed light on certain features of music, but can never elicit the specific nature of music's spatiality, the reason being that their sustenance is mainly derived from the sense of vision and its structuring capacity for orientation in the world around us, capacity for measuring and calculating it. Since we are speaking of the spatiality of music, we must also consider the sense of hearing. Does our capacity for taking in the outside world through our ears also include possibilities of experiencing other dimensions of existence than those we have been addressing hitherto? Can tone and music teach us anything about the possibilities of space?

* * *

Space presupposes delimitation. This is usually achieved by means of walls, ceiling and floor, and another limitation by sky and horizon. We can ask ourselves what there is outside the home or the edge of the forest and beyond the horizon. These questions stir the imagination and can inspire imaginative answers, of which art and philosophy afford copious examples. Earlier we discussed different relations between space and music, but all the time the common factor has been delimitation: the positioning of music within spaces with different functions and, accordingly, differing relations to their surroundings, *or* music's own delimitation upwards and downwards and its varying degree of density/sparseness. The term "floating space" appears in such a context almost self-contradictory, because delimitation by definition is evanescent. Nonetheless, Victor Zuckerkandl in *Sound and Symbol* builds his entire argument on this concept, making it the vehicle of music's claim to reality, as hinted at in the title of the German version, *Die Wirklichkeit der Musik*. Like Jacques Handschin, Zuckerkandl plays an important role in the present work, though combined, I hope, with a certain critical distance.

In addition to mathematical-physical and experienced space, Zuckerkandl propounds a third concept of space which is very much akin to the dancing space presented in an earlier chapter. Heraclitus-like, he maintains that it "flows". What do we take "floating space" to mean? It can hardly be virtual space, because it shapes the traditional rooms and spaces in both the everyday and cosmic dimensions, but only as a play to the eye, an illusion. If anything it is a space which loses itself in the depth and distance but which at the same time surrounds us, wraps itself solely around us and affects us. Arguably, it is a play to the ear and thus virtual by nature. But the difference is that, unlike the spaces of the eye and touch, it lacks correlates in so-called reality and is thus its own reality, inimitable and non-reproducible. There we have the difference, already made clear in the first chapter, between sound and tone. The former can be located in the experience spare, at least approximately, and the sound source is most often identifiable.

Sound tells us something about the nature of reality. Not so with tone. The sound source as such may be identifiable from its timbre, we hear the difference between voice and instrument and between different types of voice and instrumental timbre, especially if we can see the people producing the tone. And yet these possibilities of recognition and location are secondary in relation to other properties of tone which clearly come forward in a listener situation with no visual elements. Tone comes towards us from outside and thus is spatial in character. Not only is it present in the space outside us, it also creates its own space where it is present everywhere and nowhere. In a word: space floats.

This situation was illustrated earlier by Gregorian melody, which seems to create around itself a space of its very own with no delimitations. That example shows tones appearing in sequence, successively. But when several tones sound all at once, simultaneously, this does not result in their displacing one another or taking up different positions in space, nor, unlike colours, in their merging to form a nuance of their own. No, each and every one of them fills the space and is at the same time distinct and clearly distinguishable. They penetrate each other. In the words of the natural scientist Ernst Mach: "Why do three tones form a triad and not a triangle?" (*Sound and Symbol*, p. 297). A question which will be answered presently.

Floating space, then, is a space surrounding and flowing in towards us from all directions, in a manner of speaking similar to Stockhausen's spherical room but without its delimitations. Space is limitless and appears to lose itself in the distance and in the depth and height. It is no vacuum but a living space that invites participation, integration. Where the eye stresses distance, the ear stresses nearness, amalgamation. It is a space which has come to life. Floating space has neither order nor structure but can acquire it through man's ordering ear, his form of perception. Zuckerkandl maintains that the structure is in the tones themselves, that through their very nature they relate to each other, that they are states rather than places. I agree with his view of the properties of tones but look for the reason elsewhere, namely in the form of presentation which has just been mentioned, in man's capacity for transcendence.

Let us now return to Ernst Mach's proposition, formulated as a question, that three tones form a triad and not a triangle. However self-evident this may seem, we can still ask why it is so. The answer lies in the different categories of space which are juxtaposed. The triangular space belongs to mathematical-physical space, with its clear indication of place and distance. The triad space, by contrast, has no fixed positions in space and is instead three states in space or perhaps indeed three spatial states. Here space is transformed from the eye's distinguishing of place and distance to the ear's perception of distance in space, a state which is experienced as dynamic, as a fluctuation between equilibrium and imbalance. States are in progress towards or away from another state, i. e. from one "everywhere" to another "everywhere". State, unlike place, is directional. As Zuckerkandl puts it: "multiplicity of places and multiplicity of states, juxtaposition and interpenetration, local relation and directional relation, dynamic relation; order by places and positions that we see and touch, order of directed states of tension, dynamic order that we hear: triangles and triads, geometry and music" (*Sound and Symbol*, p. 303).

A digression forces itself upon us. We have spoken of states being in progress, in motion. The classical philosopher Zeno gained notoriety for his paradoxes, in which he denies the possibility of movement. He does this, it will be recalled, by dissecting a body's movement into different stages and asserting that at every such stage the body is in a state of rest. And so movement, he maintains, is impossible, an illusion. Zeno could perhaps have done with musical experience, so as to realise that movement is a state, indivisible and complete in itself. An example of the hazards of philosophy unaided by the fount of knowledge called music.

What is the meaning of movement? In geometric space the elementary movement of a body is a straight line, in floating space it is a tone scale. Both phenomena, in their several ways, enlighten us concerning the order of the room concerned. If a body moves through geometric space in a straight line or otherwise, the space remains unaffected and intact, while at the same time being described. If on the other hand tones move through the floating space, the space is pulled into the process, becoming a part of it. The order of the tones becomes the order of the space, as is most clear apparent from the scale of tones. This can vary in nature, include a varying number of tones and intervals, which in turn can be grouped in various ways. Zuckerkandl exemplifies with the aid of the 7-tone, diatonic scale, from which he chooses the major scale we are so familiar with. This is distinguished, not by different pitches coming one after the other but by the intervals between them being dynamic, having a direction. The pitches become tone qualities and the step or interval between them both a chronological and a spatial phenomenon. Thus viewed, the major scale becomes the image of a clear and pregnant order in which the first half moves away from the starting point while the second half moves towards the destination, the concluding tone which proves to be the octave above or below the starting tone.

The octave itself occupies a key role in floating space, through its combination of distance and amalgamation. In *Pythagoras' Sträng* I have dwelt on the significance of the octave and, not least, on its problematisation in connection with the collapse of established tonality and the emergence of atonality in 20th century Western music, viewing all this in relation to the spatiality of music. There the emphasis was on the unique character of the octave, and there was a clear fascination with it as a phenomenon. That fascination lives on, but here and now the emphasis will be on other aspects, following on from our earlier discussion of the scale and its inherent character of motion. The distinctive feature of a scale is that every tone in it has an octave replica, which means that the direction of space has, not just one centre but several, depending on the octave pitch. Thus within the audible register there are a very large – perhaps infinite – number of such centres. On the basis of the scale, one could argue that the floating space of music is traversed by force fields ebbing to and fro in perpetual oscillation: the movement from tonic to octave, which is not just a higher – or lower – tone but the movement's destination. The further away we move, the closer we come to the point of departure, a fact suggestive of the spatial character of tone and scale, or rather: the structure of the entire audible space. Where the physical field extends uniformly throughout the space, the force fields of tones are reproduced from octave to octave, resembling the perspective obtained in a hall of mirrors, where the objects viewed become progressively smaller while still retaining their characteristics. The undulating movements of floating space could also be interpreted as a rhythmic phenomenon, and the string theory of physical space could be matched in floating space by a wave theory in which the sound wave of each individual tone has been expanded to vast dimensions.

* * *

Space devoid of content is called a vacuum. In the everyday run of things we simply refer to any gap between one object and the next as an empty or vacant space. Wasted effort can be referred to in Swedish as "striking at empty air". A vacuum, thus regarded, is something with no resistance, something eluding our influence and at the same time affording us a certain freedom of movement.

Broadening our perspective to cosmic dimensions, outer space, our everyday concept of empty space is turned into something black, frightening, dizzying. We know that space contains milky ways, solar systems and black holes and that the distances between them are incomprehensible. But we need not be only frightened by the dimensions, we can also, like Giordano Bruno, allow ourselves to be inspired by them, filled with euphoria at the thought of the conceivable worlds in this immeasurable universe. It cannot be grasped by our senses like everyday space, but it can by our imagination, and so this form of empty space comes close to art and philosophy.

Is the concept of vacuum at all relevant to the floating space of music? Floating space differs from other spaces in that there is no difference between the space and the body present within it. Music creates its own space, a space which is inconceivable without the music actually sounding. "Body" and "space" coincide. If the vacuum concept is to have any meaning in this context, it must mean the negation of music, i.e. silence. But this is not just any silence. On the contrary, it is charged with music's possibility, derives its quality from that which sounds and lives in symbiosis with it. A few examples now follow of ways in which tone and silence work together, thereby elevating the total effect of both.

We have all experienced the silence preceding a concert, when the murmur of conversation in the audience subsides and the leader raises his bow and points to the oboist, who gives the tuning tone of one-line *a*. As yet this is not the actual music but its forecourt, the premonition that something is about to happen. After the orchestra have finished tuning, a murmuring silence descends on the auditorium, broken by the applause accompanying the conductor's entry. Dead silence then follows, as musicians and audience concentrate and prepare themselves for the sound to come, for merger with the floating space of music. The silence prepares us for what is to come, becomes part of it, a precondition for being able to comprehend in the first place what is going on, a species of frame or delimitation of floating space.

If the work which is being performed has more than one movement, as for example in the case of a symphony, silence descends between the movements, a silence informed by the recollection of the preceding movement, which in turn can hint at what is to follow. If, on the other hand, the work is at an end, a different kind of silence occurs – disregarding the thunderous applause which we hope the orchestra has received on the conductor putting down his baton. The silence which now reigns – we may presume – is replete with memories of what has just been sounding. The floating space remains in the representation, but probably fades away quickly. The vacuum of music takes over and in its entirety presents clearly emotional traits: waiting, expectancy sometimes rising to excitement, relief, a sense of loss. The vacuum delimits the floating space with a "not yet" and a "no longer" respectively.

Up till now we have been speaking of vacuum – empty space – as silence, But there is another term pinning down what this is all about, namely "pause" or "rest". Without these, music could not exist. These intermissions are basically of two kinds: appealing and informing. The former kind is epitomised by the general pause, i. e. all instruments falling silent, which is often highly dramatic. The drama consists in the sudden interruption and the music then continuing from a different, unexpected point of departure, as for example in Bach's *St. Matthew Passion,* the penultimate section of Part I (no. 33 *Sind Blitze und Donner in Wolken verschwunden*). We have a variant of this in a series of one or more tones separated by rests, the drama being eventually married to information concerning the musical structure, as for example at the beginning of Carl Nielsen's *Sinfonia Espansiva* and the end of Sibelius's fifth symphony. In the first mentioned, the same tone is spread out with increasing density over several octaves, i. e. the rests in between become progressively shorter until finally they cease to exist, opening out into a continuous motion, the implication being that this is where the music begins in earnest. In the second case, on the other hand, a continuous movement leads up to a general pause, after which we have a series of chords with silences of equal length in between. The rest between the last two chords is somewhat shorter, thereby signalling something new. The music marks its own termination, and in the silence which follows we can, in our mind's ear, still hear the chain of chords and understand their function, namely that of concluding the composition.

Rests of this kind mingle the appealing with the informative, but there are pauses which are solely informative, which have something essential to say about the structure of a composition or indeed a style of music. Igor Stravinsky clearly illustrates this point, above all in works composed between the 1920s and 1950s, during what is commonly termed his Neo-Classical period. Starting with *Symphonies of Wind Instruments* and continuing all the way to the ballet *Agon*, his music has one consistent feature: the flow of it is frequently punctuated by brief, almost unnoticeable rests for the whole ensemble/orchestra. This may be partly to do with ballet music bulking large in Stravinsky's output and the rests being dictated by choreographic considerations. But this is contradicted by the same property also appearing in works devoid of choreographic connections, such as *Symphony of Psalms, Concerto 'Dumbarton Oaks'* and *Symphony in Three Movements*. Here, then, we have a stylistic trait of Stravinsky's which makes him instantly recognisable. In the midst of all its rhythmic verve, the music takes on a strangely "jerky" quality, the machine seems to get stuck at irregular intervals. Something puppet-like has been inferred from this, and the observation has been made that in several of Stravinsky's works man is in fact regarded as helplessly trapped in the net of destiny. However apt such a reference may be, for present purposes we are interested in another aspect: the rest, the silence, the empty space. They are anything but appealing, have no great emotional impact. But they insinuate themselves into the process, disrupting and perforating it. The floating space of music is permeated by an empty space which breaks through or is just hinted at for brief moments, imparting both lightness and translucence to what is audible. One could describe this process as a symbiosis between floating space and empty space, and this symbiosis can be taken one step further.

When considering the *glissando* phenomenon, we remarked on its character of shapelessness and indeed its caricature of the world of tones and intervals. Outlines are all that remain of floating space. The sharp outlining of the tones, on the other hand, causes certain sections of the audible register to be left out. The tonal scale presents a clear picture: whatever the configuration of the tones, they are separated by an interstice where nothing exists, an empty space. It seems as though empty space and floating space are each other's prerequisites, as if tone and silence were two sides of the same thing. Thus the examples of rests/pauses in music quoted previously could be generalised by saying that they are only special instances of the great silence permeating music, which is a precondition for its sounding at all.

Tone and silence, then, are both antipodes and allies. But are there intermediate situations, situations where they converge, borrow properties from each other? One phenomenon which we have ignored so far is that of intensity, i.e. whether music is loud or soft. Usually there is a play between these properties, known to us through the terms *forte* and *piano* and the transitions between them, which can be sudden or gradual. On the other hand it is less common for a work of music to be very loud or very soft all the time. In the first named instance there are no space-philosophical complications, but these can occur in music which, with only few exceptions, remains all the time *pianissimo*. Luigi Nono's string quartet entitled *Fragmente-Stille, An Diotima*, written in 1980, is a vivid case in point. The name Diotima occurs in Plato's *Symposium*, where it belongs to a priestess who, Socrates maintains, taught him the nature of love. Much later the name is used by Friedrich Hölderlin with reference to his beloved and figures frequently in his poetry. Nono has inscribed the quartet score with various quotations from poems by Hölderlin, indicating an inward, conceptual link intended by the composer between poetry and music, which in turn is probably expressive of his great admiration for, and possibly identification with, the poet. Is his string quartet perhaps tacitly dedicated to Hölderlin's memory?

The first half of the title plunges us right into the theme now under consideration: "Fragment – silence". The work last for about 35 minutes, and throughout that time there are very few continuous sections of any considerable length. Otherwise we hear individual tones of varying duration, with or without *crescendo* or *diminuendo*, short outbursts from all instruments simultaneously, often quickly toned down and often employing a special playing technique in which timbre is asserted at the expense of pitch. Fragment and silence condition one another, are inconceivable without each other. The sounding sections are purely fragmentary, displaying little in the way of movement, direction or interconnection. In addition, as mentioned earlier, when the music sounds it does so almost invariable with a soft dynamic, i. e. is barely audible, bordering on silence. To say that tone and silence are symbiotically related in this work is only a half-truth. What is still more important is that silence envelops the entire music, is a superior phenomenon. Nono balances here on the boundary between the floating space of music and empty space, the latter vibrating from the former, which in turn gives us a glimpse of a world without music.

Tone and Music

In the argument so far, the words "tone" and "music" have been used interchangeably, implying an assumption that the two phenomena are so closely bound up with one another that no comment is called for. On closer reflection, though, uncertainty arises as to whether the nature of tone is wholly absorbed by that of music, and vice versa. Let us problematise the interrelationship of these two phenomena with the aid of the following statement, coupled with a question.

Music consists of tones. Do tones consist of music?

The statement seems like a truism. Of course music consists of tones, music is indisputably a tone art. We will leave it at that for the time being and now turn to consider the question of whether the tone contains music. Putting it drastically, does one single tone amount to music? The answer depends on the length of the tone: the longer its duration, the more easily we perceive the specifically musical qualities which make possible the existence of music – always assuming a duration which does not degenerate into literal monotony. In an earlier chapter we fantasised on the subject of how our remotest ancestors experienced their first confrontation with a tone and how they tried to find new tones. People have undoubtedly experienced the musicality of tone in this notional scenario, and we are of course free to go on speculating in the same direction, but perhaps a more fruitful path to follow is that of existing music in which a single, sustained tone is the central process. By way of example I have chosen the last two minutes of the Swedish composer Ingvar Lidholm's *Poesis* for orchestra, written in 1964.

The section consists of one long, sustained tone, more exactly one-line *b-flat*, which begins *pianissimo* and then gradually grows louder. En route, the timbre successively changes, beginning with the horns. They are relieved by woodwinds and the violins intervene. Eventually the heavier brass instruments – trumpet and trombone – join in the colouring of the tone, and we now understand why the composer has opted one-line *b -flat*: this tone can be played on most instruments, which maximises the possible variation of timbre. The whole of this section can be seen as a study in a tone's changeability, how it can be orchestrated. But it is also an example of the way in which a sustained tone moves. The gradual crescendo means the tone coming closer and closer to the unbearable. What we experience here is the materiality of the tone turning into expression. This is especially clear when the shattering timbre of the trumpets comes into play, which in turn leads to the conclusion: the tone is split up and the shards of timbre rain down, followed by silence.

"Threatening danger, fear, catastrophe" are the titles Arnold Schoenberg has given to the three sections of his *Accompaniment to a cinematographic scene,* and this would be a perfectly possible interpretation of the sustained tone in Lidholm's work. Catastrophe is made manifest not least when the tone simply explodes. This interpretation is reinforced by a corresponding point in Alban Berg's opera *Wozzeck*, where all through the murder scene one tone is sustained, hidden by all the other things happening in the music. After the deed has been done, that tone remains in two long *crescendi* from the orchestra, the first of which leads up to an explosion from the percussion. Lidholm himself has opened the door to this possible interpretation by prefacing the sustained tone with a double bass solo in which the distinctive timbre of the instrument, not least in its high registers, conveys the impression of speech – pleading, insistent, perhaps desperate. *Poesis*, then, would seem to end in a scene of music drama without words.

The conclusion one can draw from this discussion is that tones actually consist of music, that a single tone can contain a good deal more than that single tone. Our exemplification has employed music which in some way has dramatic inflections, but other music too can illuminate the fact of tones being big with music. The beginning of Anton Bruckner's ninth symphony demonstrates this to the point of overstatement: a barely audible tone fills the room, concentrates it in its timbre and makes it lie, aura-like, round about it. The tone radiates space, reinforced by the special tinge achieved by the *tremolo* playing of the strings. The motion reinforces the space. As yet we are unable to place this tone in a wider context, it has just broken the silence and established an indeterminate, floating, indeed mysterious space. Apart from the tone repetition, the motion is minimal. The first sign of something in the offing comes from the wind instruments diffidently intoning the same tone, followed by the minor third above. This hints at a minor tonality, reinforced by the next deviation from the sustained tone – the fifth above. These movements, however, are small compared with what is just about to happen. The sustained tone gathers strength, comes closer and suddenly bifurcates to the tones immediately above and below it – a musical cell division, one might say. In its tonal context, this is a dramatic occurrence: within the space of a few bars the music goes from D minor to G sharp major, a very big leap and, in terms of the cycle of fifths, the furthest possible distance away from the starting point. The tone has been pregnant with other tones and it now opens out like a flower to give birth to them. The space is no longer an effect of the tone's radiation, aura, but now also becomes tangible, direct. The door is flung wide open, revealing a room both huge and delimited; movement becomes space. The effect on the listeners is very powerful; the dusky nuances and subdued colouring of the opening bars are unexpectedly shot through by a dark, incandescent light, which, however, fades.

 How is this to be understood? Bruckner's music inviting flights of fancy and formulations verging on metaphysics is one thing. Pondering them rationally is another. Returning for a moment to *Poesis*, we can note that the living force characterising the sustained tone emanates from the perpetual shifts of timbre, i. e. from each individual moment being dominated by different overtones with different mixes. In principle, every tone has an infinite number of overtones, as is the case, then, with Bruckner's long sustained tone. Its infinite content manifests itself in the parturition of quite different tones, in its giving birth to music. The overtones are projected downwards to fundamental tones which surround the starting tone, a conceivable but perhaps somewhat farfetched scenario. Nonetheless, the effect is that retrospectively the sustained tone is experienced as full of other tones which are only waiting to be allowed to manifest themselves. The only plausible conclusion is an affirmative answer to the question with which we began: tones consist of music, are filled with other tones. *Expansion is the tone's form of existence.*

Common to all these examples, and especially *Poesis* and *Wozzeck*, is their predication of a context in which their specific design has a characterising function, their breaking free of an otherwise "many-toned" ambience. But there is music which does not predicate this multi-tonality but, on the contrary, takes a single tone as its starting point. Giacinto Scelsi makes an illuminating example. This Italian composer, who lived between 1905 and 1988, takes meditation over and exploration of a single tone, varying from one work to another, as his compositional principle. "Through rhythmisations and varying modes of performance, by shifting timbre but also by stretching pitch, Scelsi creates a continuum out of the thematic tone. (...) The sound body Scelsi evolved was ever-changing, trembling and drilling, sliding and shimmering. Timbre was a beginning with no fixed end point" (Wallrup, p. 25). This quotation comes from an essay on *Stimmung* in the broadest sense of the word, drawing a parallel between Scelsi's absorption by the individual tone and Bruckner's and Beethoven's (ninth symphony) absorption by a species of "ur-timbre". Once again we find ourselves nearing the territory of mysticism, which is not alien to Jacques Handschin either. His mysticism, though, concerns the interaction of tones, whereas Scelsi focuses on the tone itself and shows how charged it is with musical possibilities.

But in non-Western music too, the individual tone lies at the centre of music's possibilities, as is illustrated by the repertoire for the Chinese *ch'in* (or *qin*) zither, one of China's most ancient musical instruments and girt about with metaphysical and philosophical notions. True, we are dealing here with music based on the pentatonic system and, unlike Scelsi, polytonal, but even so the (plucked) individual tone is at the centre of things. With the tonal system comprising five tones, the individual tone has the opportunity of developing, as is underlined by differing modes of performance. The seven-stringed instrument has silk strings, , which makes for a large number of nuances, ranging from open string to the most shimmering overtones, glissandi and outright tapping sounds. The tones breathe and the silence between them vibrates from the sound. There is one striking similarity between music for the *ch'in* and Scelsi's meditations: the absence of notation. More correctly, in the former case there is a kind of notation, a fret script or tablature indicating which tone is to be plucked and how, but on the other hand not any notation in the Western sense, indicating the structure and course of the music. In the latter case, on the other hand, the notation is a post facto construction to facilitate a performance, but the actual composing is done on the instrument. In early years, Scelsi could spend hours at the piano striking one and the same tone to extract from it as many nuances as possible. The mature artist sits at an untuned piano or with what is called an onioline, an electronic string instrument with keys which are played monophonically and makes possible microtones with no audible gaps between them. Thus equipped he improvises and tape-records the result. For polyphonic music, the result of the improvisation is recorded on several tapes which are combined with each other, after which the notation scribe takes over and tries to pin down the result in writing.

It is clear from these procedures that music putting the individual tone at the centre of things is not necessarily dependent on notation. Composition proceeds in a different way and subject to other conditions. But tone can also have a function other than being a musical statement in splendid isolation. If the process is a rapid one we get a host of, possibly innumerable, tones interacting. The tone is then turned into a vehicle of music, a necessary but not sufficient precondition for music. The need then arises for a notation which will make performance possible and elucidate the structure. This will be an important theme presently, but first we are going to put two questions concerning the relation between tone and music.

Are all tones music? And conversely: *Is all music tones?*

On closer reflection one soon realises that the answer to the first question – whether all tones are music – has to be negative. Our previous discussion concerning the relation between tone and sound has shown beyond any doubt that the all-embracing world of sound contains tones of many different kinds which cannot reasonably be classed as music. The musically charged tone is something different from and more than just pitch; it hints at a context.

If the first question is an easy one to answer, the answer to the second will admittedly be simple, but as a consequence we gain a complex picture of music in general. Here again, the straight answer is negative: not all music is tones, or, more exactly, not all music is only tones. The latter are articulated by the phenomenon of rhythm, the world of rhythm and the world of tone penetrate each other, condition each other, enter into a symbiotic relationship. And what is more, rhythm can emancipate itself from tone, lead a life of its own and exist independently of tone, as is the case among certain African peoples. Nonetheless, we regard this phenomenon as music, which would thus seem to consist of tone, including timbre and nuance, and also of rhythm or time value, including intimated pitch, timbre and nuance.

How can we conceive of the relation between tone and rhythm? Here we have to turn our ear away from their degree of amalgamation and towards their degree of incompatibility. We recall the music of Giacinto Scelsi and music for the Chinese *ch'in* zither. What strikes us is the absence here of distinct rhythms and strong accents. In this respect these examples resemble the melodies of Gregorian chant, in which the rhythmic element is very discreet and the music designed to illuminate the sacred words of the liturgy solely with the aid of tones. This situation is in fact reminiscent of early man and his notional first encounter with musical tone. He *contemplates* it in the same way as in the Catholic liturgy, with Scelsi and in music for the *ch'in*. Thus the essential thing for tone would seem to be meditation, introversion, beholding – a philosophic attitude, if you will. One lets go of oneself in a way that is ostensibly passive. Rhythm, by contrast, is active, impelling. It wants something from tone, wants to organise it, take possession of it and force it into action. Here we can hark back to Handschin's antithesis, quoted earlier, between art as a contemplation of proportions and art as an outflow of the emotional. Tone stands forth here as the given norm, while rhythm becomes the will to attack that norm and limit its scope. One might say: objectivity versus subjectivity.

Fully realising that there are many intermediate positions in the relation between tone and rhythm, I have chosen here to dramatise the antithesis between them. This is partly for a pedagogical purpose, that of clarifying two different phenomena and attitudes connected with them which, if the line of thought is pursued long enough, can become irreconcilable. And partly because music exists which radically presents this antagonism. I refer to the first culmination of polyphony in the circle of Notre Dame in Paris, which moreover prompts a number of other deliberations material to the ongoing discussion.

* * *

"Let us in our imagination go to a service in Notre Dame in about 1200 and listen to the music. First we hear the choir singing an excerpt from one of the songs in the mass which not only adorns the act of worship but *is* an essential part of it – a gradual, for example. The melody rises and falls in a calm, steady rhythm, blossoming forth into melismas. It seems to create an imaginary room around itself, seems to be more than the gentle flow of tones. Suddenly it comes to rest on a tone which is sustained, above this sustained tone from the choir we hear a soloist singing a melody with a distinct rhythmic profile: short-long, short-long, long, long-short, long-short, long. The imaginary room is transformed into a real room delimited by the upper and lower voice and reinforced by the resonance. At certain points the choir changes tone, but stays on the new tone as if on a musical floor. After a while the soloist pauses while the choir continues with its calmly fluid melody. Once again it is suspended on a sustained tone above which, this time, two or three soloists sing a rhythmically profiled section having the same rhythm in all voices, while the purely melodic movement is independent, although with a close distance of the others. The result is an energetically forward-moving music in the which the real room begins to be filled out. The choir then continues with its melody as though nothing had happened and in turn launches into a section in which the sustained tone expected instead enters into a rhythmic symbiosis with the other parts, the onward-thrusting movement pulls all the music along with it. Finally we hear, for the last time, the solitary choral melody rounding off this part of the service. What we have witnessed is a procession within the liturgy, the importance and meaning of which are highlighted by the lavish musical *mise-en-scène*." (*Europa i Musiken*, pp. 23–24)

There are several ways of relating to this imagined moment in the past. One that instantly springs to mind is to emphasise, like musicology, the new and prefiguring aspects of this repertoire. Starting with the renewal aspect, we note that, for the first time in the history of polyphony, we encounter the names of two composers: Leonin and Perotin. Music acquires a face and we sense an individuality. Furthermore, the contrast between the long, sustained tones and the rhythmically vigorous upper voices suggests a variety of influences within one and the same music – on the one hand ecclesiastical, in the form of the Gregorian chorale, and on the other a popular influence in the form of dance ballads. The upper voice dances along, as it were, and we are reminded that Paris at this time was becoming an international melting pot, a role often played by big cities. Marxist-minded music historians have been disposed to see these various influences as the embodiment of class conflicts, with the amalgamation of the intrinsically incompatible leading to a stylistic synthesis, literally com-position (*Geschichte als Weg zum Musikverständnis*, pp. 233–250).

But we can also adopt a different approach, namely that of keeping things in proportion, in that the people of the time do not appear to have been properly aware of the revolution which musicology has ascribed to them. A latter-day listener must concede that they are in the right, and this is not only connected with the distance in time circumscribing our chances of hearing fundamental differences. The fact of polyphony having evolved from Gregorian chant and, to begin with at least, taken over its melodic and rhythmic behaviour, is no less important. In the notional listener situation presented above, it is not only the contrast but also the continuity that is decisive. The upper voices seem to grow out of the Gregorian tilth, recede and then gather speed again. The new always reverts to the old, they enter into a close union and the task of the new is to impart brilliance to the old. The first polyphony is festive music in honour of Gregorian chant and to the glory of God. The fact that this chant can be subjected to pretty rough treatment, with a single tone being endlessly stretched out beyond any melodic connection, is not indicative of disrespect. The series of sustained tones remains the beginning and end of everything, and the name eventually given to these long tones is a characterisation: *cantus firmus*, fixed song. This fixed, given melody would, in the course of evolution, be emancipated from its ecclesiastical starting point, in two respects: the melody could be of secular/popular origin and the method of composition itself developed into sophisticated techniques such as the isorhythmic motet of the 14th century and the cantus firmus mass of the 15th and 16th centuries. Gregorian chant went on leading a life of its own side by side with the development of polyphony, with the result that it became a subject of innovation and creativity well into the 15th century. Only after that did it exclusively assume the role of a venerated branch of the tree of European music, and in our own time it has attracted renewed interest as a source of artistic experience.

This lengthy argument began with the question of whether all music is tones. The answer has proved to be negative, with the positive rider that music is both tone and rhythm. But our example from the early 13th century also shows with razor-sharp clarity the near-paradigmatic contrast between the two, a contrast redolent of drama and with implications for the philosophy of music. I have previously assumed that the reason for our hearing both space and movement in music is to be found in our form of representation in the Kantian sense, but the fundamental importance of rhythm in music enjoins a tentative rethink. Rhythm in general and dance rhythms in particular, after all, are closely bound up with bodily movement: one marches in step, marks time and moves regularly, one way or another, in the whirl of the dance. This bodily activity is then transferred to music which we only listen to and which we here in motion and perhaps in space. The transfer could be termed metaphorical, as it is by Roger Scruton (*The Aesthetics of Music*, pp. 91–92), and also be applicable to the floating space of music, which could then be presumed to have acquired this property by transfer from the non-directional space of dancing. This will have to remain an open question for the time being.

The development of Western music has been hinted at, both in this chapter and in the one before it. That development depends on a notation which rhythmically regulates the interaction of the voices. And so we have the emergence of what is termed mensural notation, on which modern notation is founded. Composition and notation proceed hand in hand, and their combined possibilities begin to be perceived: one and the same music can in future be spread out over time and space, because it will be repeatable by other musicians than the original ones. One senses genres and work concepts in their cradle, and music as an autonomous art.

Sharpening the historical perspective still further, polyphony is not exclusive to Western music. On the contrary, the phenomenon of two or more tones sounding at once is well-known among both "primitive" and "civilised" peoples in large parts of the world, specially in Asia and Oceania. It is an improvisatory performing practice handed down aurally and often producing complex results. This type of music is familiar to us from geographically closer quarters through the famous Georgian examples, with their polyphony and long, sustained tones. Western polyphony, however, is distinguished by its symbiosis with notation and, consequently, its increasingly prominent element of thoroughgoing organisation. Once again, the development of music influences notation, at the same time as the latter points to new possibilities for music. All great cultures are written cultures, but only the Western European one has brought forth a *musical written culture*. This has a history amounting to the successive realisation of inherent possibilities, from the first hesitant experiments to the climax almost a thousand years later. With this formulation we have introduced an element of Platonism into the relation between tone and music, an aspect which we will now turn to consider.

* * *

We will begin with the antithesis between *discovery* and *invention*, its application to European/Western musical development and its manifestations of floating space. The alternatives will be contrasted, elaborated, modified and perhaps problematised, in which process a certain reiteration of viewpoints already stated will be unavoidable, at the same time as I hope that the statement of the problem will be deepened into the bargain. We will begin with the emergence of polyphony in the 11th and 12th centuries. Homophonic Gregorian chant prevailed, and in addition to that one could indulge in interjections and additions to the established repertoire – tropes, as they were called – which could also occur simultaneously with the pre-existing melody. Notation also existed and its function was mnemotechnical – an aid to memory in managing an increasingly copious melodic repertoire. At some point during these centuries, one or two musicians/composers will, independently of each other, put down in notation, in writing, a counterpart which has not sounded before. Notation then serves, not exclusively or primarily as an aid to memory but as a *means for creating something new.* This is a revolutionary step, a kind of musical declaration of independence. For the first time in history, a musical written culture now appears, in contradistinction to sporadic essays in that direction by other high civilisations. Out of this written culture emerges the whole of the phenomenon which we call Western music.

Is polyphony fixed in writing as a means of creating something new a discovery or an invention? If it were a discovery, this would mean that the phenomenon, like the ideas of Plato, had existed previously and was just waiting to be made visible. Now, as mentioned earlier, music had already employed polyphony previously, often as improvisation. The new development the putting down of things in writing and the primacy of writing. These things, *per* se, had existed as abstract possibilities, perhaps as "ideas" in the Platonic sense, far earlier, but had not been "discovered" until the 11th and 12th centuries. The fact of polyphonic music existing before the creative possibilities of notation began to be explored leads one to conclude that musical script is an invention generating discoveries.

Another factor which can shed light on the relation between discovery and invention is the choice of intervals in polyphony, intervals which sound simultaneously, thereby imparting a basic character to the music. The first fully developed, previously described polyphony in about 1200 is distinguished by a harmony in which – apart, of course, from the octave – fourths and fifths predominate. Other intervals such as seconds and thirds are experienced more as shading, perhaps disturbances underscoring the basically harmonic character of the music. In about 1400 a development sets in which, two hundred years later, has put the third at the centre of things as an all-permeating harmonic force, with the earlier intervals having more or less the character of a framework. The third, of course, had always been known, but its harmonic potential had been ignored. From that which is already present, possibilities are audibly elicited which have not been regarded hitherto, and are transformed from latent to manifest phenomena. Into the bargain we get the major triad, which is emancipated, so to speak, in the 17th and 18th centuries and acquires an independent, fundamental standing in Western music.

Thus far one could say that the use of the third is primarily an invention and the major triad a virtually logical consequence of it. But the situation is complicated by this triad occurring naturally, in a tone's series of partials and its first six tones. True, we do not hear these tones as a triad, but we do hear them as a timbre imparting colour to the tone. All the same, the agreement between human combination and acoustic foundation is a striking one, tempting us to assume that the triad – and with it the third as a harmony-founding interval – has been discovered, all the more so as the overtone phenomenon was discovered in the 17th century, i.e. at the same time as the emancipated triad was becoming more and more important.

A third factor is spelt *tonality*, meaning a central tone governing a musical process for longer or shorter distances. This is exemplified by what we term keys, with their two tonal clans of major and minor, in which it is indeed the triad which makes the running. In fact, following on from Jean-Philippe Rameau, one could define tonality by the three basic chords which are the spinal cord of its classical Western structure: tonic, dominant and subdominant. But the history of tonality extends a long way back in time. Leaving aside the forms it assumes in extra-European music cultures and confining ourselves to our own cultural circle, we already find an embryo in the music of and around Notre Dame. We recall the long, sustained tones round which the counter-voices develop. One sustained tone is exchanged for another at irregular intervals, and when the section has been completed, a progression appears from tone to tone which, in its infancy, describes changes of a central tone, i.e. a tonality as described above. This is clearly audible in the music, and we experience a progression from one state to another. We hear movement.

Six hundred years later, during a number of decades round about 1800, the development which began in Notre Dame has achieved completion and the music has realised its inherent tendencies. It has undergone a process of rationalisation (Max Weber: *The Rational and Social Foundations of Music*): instead of eight modes we get two tonal families – major and minor – from an intermittently intricate polyphonic structure there comes a reduction to, essentially, three chords, i.e. those described by Rameau, instead of a complex, irregular rhythmic structure a regular grouping of bars and time signatures emerges, instead of the motley flora of music pieces with all manner of titles, a work concept is established containing a handful of genres – opera, lied, symphony, sonata, quartet. Historical development – or rather, an interpretation of history – leads to what we call Viennese Classicism, something which will inform our perception of music for years to come.

Once more we have to ask ourselves, is this development a voyage of discovery or a stalwart labour of invention? One's first impulse might be to declare, Solomon-like: both, because a discovery too is preceded by hard work. This would simplify matters for us and perhaps relieve us of various disturbing metaphysical tendencies. Nevertheless I prefer the metaphysical path, my reason being that invention is not governed by chance. A species of unconscious idea concerning the direction of the invention, crassly speaking, its usefulness for the actual idea, is just as important. Direction can uncover context, reveal something hitherto unknown. In short: one discovers. This thought can be given one more twist into a Platonic perspective which has already been hinted at. Thus Peter Kivy, for example, discusses the possibility of a work of music having already existed as a Platonic idea, quite irrespective of whether it is realised or not (*Platonism in Music*, pp. 45–47). The composer's work consists in laying bare this idea, or as Schiller puts it, *Eine dunkle, mächtige Totalidee* (cit. Susanne Langer: *Feeling and Form*, p. 120).

The task is to make the idea comprehensible to the sensory world, which direction the activity of compositional invention should take, what the representation as a whole looks like, to have a premonition of the actual idea. But – are we not then saying that this idea has an independent existence, independently of the author? This is so in a manner of speaking, namely when the idea sounds like a work. Then the author's task is done and the work leads a life of its own. But there at the same time we have the weak point of the notion of the idea of the work existing before the composer has even hit on the thought of writing it down. A work can be performed in various ways and with widely differing interpretations. In that case, which one is to rank as the Platonic idea? This question opens the way to a discussion of a work's ontological status, its form of being. Very much has been written on this subject, but the most important viewpoint to my mind relativises the work concept, transforming it into a historical phenomenon with a beginning, a heyday and perhaps a dissolution (Lydia Goehr: The *Imaginary Museum of Musical Works*).

If the notion of a work already existing in Plato's world of ideas before being translated into sounding coin thus leaves a number of questions unanswered, this need not be the case with the development of Western music as it has been outlined here. The properties highlighted there are a good deal more general than those of a work of music: successive or simultaneous tone sequences, choice of intervals, tone system, rhythmic structure. Viewing our musical history as an ongoing laying-bare of a Platonic idea is perhaps a not altogether common perspective, but it is perfectly possible. Take the phenomenon of "motion". Its central meaning, of course, is movement from one place or position to another place/position, with starting point and end point as the frame of movement, its distance, interval. We recall the music of Notre Dame and its long, sustained tones which, taken together, result in movement from central tone to central tone. Six hundred years later this process has been refined more and more, leading to what we call modulation, i. e. movement from one key to another, a very important form-creating element in the music of the 18th and 19th centuries. Modulation conveys an impression of movement, but other elements also contribute: the combination of rhythm-metre-tempo, crescendo-diminuendo, sudden accents and, last but not least, the thoroughgoing interaction of movement and change that permeates the music of this period. Movement seems to be built into the tone system itself, as is illustrated by the example, mentioned earlier, of the major scale which first moves away from the starting point and then moves towards it, no matter whether we mean the octave above or below. It looks as if, through the centuries, the inherent possibilities of the tonal material were increasingly laid bare until, in about 1800, their total realisation was achieved and with it the true and fundamental idea of Western music: floating space.

The juxtaposition of the "classicism" phenomenon in the history of music and ideas with the philosophical concept of "floating space" is no coincidence. Without it being spelled out, this is the precondition for Zuckerkandl's proposition of the said concept, its identification with musical classicism, the latter being understood as extending from the beginning of the 18th century to the closing years of the 19th. Thus interpreted, floating space acquires concretion and depth. It is nuanced. To Zuckerkandl, floating space is normative and the order prevailing there also sets the norm for *all* music.

It is possible, then, for the development of Western music down to the 19th century to be construed as an increasingly clear exposure of the Platonic idea of floating space. But what happens after the 19th century? How is the ensuing development to be interpreted, a development which, where art music is concerned, spells the dissolution of tonality and movement or at least its reformulation, and which is in no way congruent with the distinctive properties of the centuries immediately preceding? Zuckerkandl answers this partly by ignoring the issue and partly by asserting that a tone world not distinguished by the ordering principles of classicism lacks order. In other words, we have to investigate what in the floating space of music is conditioned by time and what can be reasonably presumed to possess absolute validity, to transcend history.

One notion which dominates Zuckerkandl's thinking is that floating space is traversed by forces, that tones attract one another. This notion is as natural in classicism, where pretty well every moment shows something beyond itself, appears to form part of an overarching scheme, as it seems dubious in Schoenberg's atonality, the absolute antipode. The "laws" of classicism is replaced by the lawlessness of atonality, and what is more, the octave loses its unifying role, even though it shows a semblance of life in twelve-tone technique, as a framework for the chromatic scale. Interval precision is superseded by the approximate – in other words, a step in the direction of the amorphous, maybe perilous world which we encounter in the phenomenon of *glissando*. Two worlds and two values collide.

Schoenberg's break-out from the floating space permeated by the play of tonality's forces has been sharply criticised, and not only from a valuation viewpoint, i. e. for the "beautiful" being supplanted by the "ugly". The turn to atonality has also been challenged on grounds of history and principle, as for example in Martin Vogel's *Schönberg und die Folgen*. Vogel takes his cue from the well-known fact of Western polyphonic music having originally built its harmony on the fifth and the fourth, until eventually it incorporated the major and minor third and put them at the centre of things, a progression matched by the first six overtones. In or around 1900, he argues, the time was ripe for going one step further by incorporating the minor seventh, i. e. the seventh overtone.

To this we can object that classical harmony already knows a chord in which the minor seventh plays a pivotal part, namely the dominant seventh chord, with its powerful kinetic energy. Even so, Vogel has a point, at least if we start with the tonal system and wish to develop it further. Usually, though, composers do not in the first instance think of drawing conclusions for the future from the prevailing tonal system: instead they use it as a given point of departure. On the other hand, they willingly draw compositional conclusions from what has already been presented by predecessors and contemporaries, which is exactly what Schoenberg was doing. His historical perspective extended some 150 years back in time, and what he saw – and heard – there was a more and more far-reaching uniformisation of the musical material, in which everything can be traced back to an initial idea. He elevated this observation to a norm, systematising it with the aid of twelve-tone technique. The thought of unity took command, thrusting the harmonic result into the background. The floating space of music was transformed from cosmos to chaos.

This is how a critique of Arnold Schoenberg's contribution can be formulated. It may seem harsh, categorical and unbalanced, but Schoenberg's music contains many more qualities than can be deduced from this harsh judgement, and so I will endeavour to nuance the picture, not least with regard to the floating space of music.

The starting point is Schoenberg's unfinished opera *Moses and Aaron* and the final scene of Act II, that outburst of helplessness and despair. After smashing the golden calf and the tablets of the law, Moses quarrels fiercely with Aaron and is put more and more on the defensive. He tries to evade the ostensibly striking truth of Aaron's assertion that not only he, Aaron, has tried to make God intelligible by mans of an image. Moses himself has described the Infinite as a burning bush and as clay tablets and writing, i.e. as something concrete, limited. Moses' and the opera's last words are: "O word, thou word that I lack!" and the entire episode is initially interspersed with the whispering speech choruses of the Israelites, which are eventually silenced by terror and confusion. All this is counterpointed in the 29 bars under consideration here by a string cantilena which performs breathtaking leaps, sometimes exceeding three octaves. The basic homophony notwithstanding, hardly anything could be further removed from Gregorian chant. On the other hand the leap does not deny its origin in the Wagnerian espressivo, but its interpretation is open to discussion. It is tempting to see this "burst" melody as representing Moses' own fragmentation, his breakdown. But another interpretation is also possible. The string cantilena pushes the rhetorical element to its furthest extreme, in true expressionist spirit. It is as though, in its intensity, it is trying to say to Moses: "Do not despair. If the word betrays you, the tones, music, remain. They are stronger, more convincing, than any number of words."

On closer inspection, this string melody proves, with few exceptions, to consist entirely of "dissonant" leaps: tritone, major sevenths, minor ninths, often spanning several octaves. Movement plays a subordinate role, except in the bar where the melody breaks down during its headlong progress towards the deep register. The remaining ten bars are a kind of echo, the melody eventually levels out and comes to rest on a long, sustained tone ending in a *crescendo – diminuendo* and extinction. The changes of nuance apply to the whole melody: one and the same tone swells and fades, often within the space of a second or so, *ff* is quickly followed by a significantly softer nuance or *vice versa*, and the string timbre endows tones and nuances with its distinctive rhetorical intensity.

How does this melody function? Do we experience the tones as participating in a reciprocal play of forces, relating to each other? The answer is not straightforward, and there are arguments both for and against. Where, exceptionally, the melody moves in steps of seconds, an impression of coherence can occur, as is also the case with repetitions of isolated tones or groups of tones. On other occasions – the overwhelming majority – the feeling of tone coherence will not come. The principle whereby pitches have been foreordained – twelve-tone technique – is too abstract and random to generate a feeling of context. Each tone can be followed by any tone whatsoever, a situation bordering on the arbitrary. Schoenberg appears to have sensed this, because he makes the tone strengths, nuances, come in as a context-creating element. Every alteration of pitch is accompanied by a change of nuance, either instantly or successively. This is especially striking whenever a tone is given a crescendo sign leading on to the next tone in a completely different register. It is as if Schoenberg seeks to conjure the tones, despite the elimination of tonality, to participate in the play of forces and be attracted by each other. As we have already argued, *crescendo* implies a rapprochement, *diminuendo* a distancing. Thus Schoenberg mobilises space and movement as means of context creation.

The elements of incoherence in this melody do not prevent us from also hearing something else. The great leaps may tear the interconnection of the tones to shreds, but at the same time they clarify the space in between them, articulate that space. Here the register takes on a meaning far transcending that which would be found if the melody had moved exclusively in an intermediate register. In the floating space of the music the tones appear in this case to be coming from different directions but, paradoxically, to be bound together through their great distance from each other. The innate force of the space brings together that which is separated, space and rhetoric united create context.

Other sections of *Moses and Aaron* can also be viewed in the light of these problems, e. g. the ghostly interlude where the people's lack of a leader grows into terror, or the orgiastic dance round the golden calf which has the same people turning into a mob. Without going any further into these sections, it is clear that Schoenberg is applying more traditional – in a word: tonal, octave-based – patterns of movement to historically new material. He moves in a no man's land between the frame intervals of major seventh/minor ninth and octave, between Einstein and Newton. Rather like Moses vis-à-vis his people, he forces the intrinsically directionless matter to submit to his will to directional movement. Both the force and the problematic in this music emanate from the conflict between mind and matter. Therein lies its drama.

* * *

Jacques Handschin, in his *Der Toncharakter*, touches on aesthetic/artistic standpoints, e. g. on pp. 83, 104 and 118. The two last mentioned are especially typical, abjuring any particular (musical) aesthetic. But this does not prevent him from feeling strongly tempted to regard homophonic music as more aesthetic than polyphonic and, eventually, chordal music (p. 83). Without in any way passing judgement on this particular valuation, one feels that Handschin is a prey to conflicting feelings. As a scholar and philosopher he aims for the utmost objectivity and balance, as a musician and listener he cannot fend off the aesthetic experience. The question we should ask ourselves is whether, against the background of Schoenberg's revolution and from the thoughts present in *Der Toncharakter*, it is possible to sift out aspects of importance for composing in our time. I believe this to be the case, but before entering into that discussion I would warn the reader that my text is going to take an autobiographical turn in which an argument of principle is based on first-hand experience. The author as philosopher steps down for a moment in deference to the author as composer.

As a young man I had a rather unusual concert experience. The then Stockholm Concert Hall Orchestra was performing Mozart's Symphony No. 38, better known as the Prague Symphony. I had studied an analysis of the symphony beforehand and was thus thoroughly prepared. I followed the course of it attentively, admiring the combination of motifs, the mastery of form – I listened analytically. Suddenly I shifted my focus and was almost bowled over by the timbre, the euphony. The brass, not least, attracted my attention. From that experience my thoughts went to that which sustains the euphony, namely tone. Carefully considered, it is rare for such an evanescent phenomenon as tone to have shown itself capable of being the kingpin of sounding structures by which we are profoundly affected. After the performance I put my reflections to the person accompanying me, and he nodded agreement. No more was said, and my train of thought eventually ebbed out.

Far later I understood that I had brushed up against a central issue in all philosophy and music: its essence or ontology. But the road to insight proved to be a long one, half a century long to be exact. The 20-year-old who, during a concert, discovered tone *an sich* and its miraculous capacity for spellbinding, had dreams of becoming a composer, dreams which were brought true in a professional career of more than 60 years duration. Some time in his thirties he meets Arnold Schoenberg and his world, an encounter which leaves a long-lasting imprint on his compositional thinking. Not that twelve-tone technique and, from there, serial technique have played such an important role – on the contrary, it was laid aside as being an unnecessary tool of artistic expression. But the overarching thought of the twelve tones' equality of status and, in that connection, the role of the octave interval became pivotal. With Schoenberg the octave has an ambivalent standing. It frames the chromatic scale of the twelve tones, but at the same time is proscribed in practical composing, this latter being connected with the bid made by Schoenberg and others to break free of the major/minor system. An understandable objective, but perhaps a little primitive in the realisation. For my own part I have tried in various ways over the years to relax and break through the octave prohibition without making a forced landing in traditional harmony.

Then there is a further circumstance. The equal status of the twelve tones has the effect of levelling out the intervals, so that it makes no difference which interval is sounding. Anything can happen and we do not know why it happens. At the same time we know that, depending on the context, tones are not equal and that intervals, accordingly, are different. We like to experience something of this difference, rather like light and shade, as opposed to lingering in a grey mist – music's equivalent of Newton's disc. Schoenberg, in my opinion, is at his most hear-worthy during his so-called middle period, with works such as *Erwartung* and *Five Pieces for Orchestra* opus 16, in which the tone combinations are still undogmatic and his sense of timbre triumphantly successful.

The compositional problem can be formulated as follows. How do you reconquer light and shade in art music without "lapsing" into uncritical use of the octave? Some might argue, perhaps, that this has already happened in minimalism, and I have a genuine admiration above all for John Adams. But since, for many reasons, I cannot disregard the modernist line in the development of art music over the past hundred years, I look instead to Dmitri Mitropoulos' formulation: "a kind of twelve-tone music filled with Ravel-like flavour and appeal" (Rudolf Reti: *Tonality, Atonality, Pantonality*, p. 119). Here Jacques Handschin's system of fifths with its Pythagorean ancestry enters the scene as a theoretical option for artistic creativity. It will be recalled how the tones are grouped by fifths in both directions, emanating from *d*. The acoustic in the form of the Pythagorean comma causes trouble, though: the circle of fifths overshoots a little, hinting at a spiral. Infinity lurks round the corner, something which Handschin seeks to avoid. For my own part, I want to do the opposite – venture forth on the infinite ocean of tones and endeavour to mark out shipping lanes and install navigation lights. The ideal is to allow the tones not only to be at loggerheads, as with Schoenberg the serialist, but, in the spirit of the tonal characters, to make them co-operate, to treat them gently and respectfully.

Paradoxically enough, Handschin himself has, without knowing it, indicated a possible way forward. He adduces the 9th century treatise *Musica Enchiriadis* and the scale presented there (*Der Toncharakter*, pp. 316–320) as evidence for the existence of a fifth-generated tonal system in earlier musical thought. The scale is given here with a special addition for my purposes: ...*GAB-flatc/defg/abc'd'/e' –f-sharp'g'a'/b'c-sharp"*...The obliques demarcate the tetrachords whose initial tones are a fifth apart. The addition lies in the surrounding points, hinting at the scale's infinite continuation both upwards and downwards. The scale thus constructed is suited to the above mentioned infinite ocean. Extended upwards and downwards, the scale comprises twelve fifths, from contra *G* to four-line *g*, a gigantic space containing no fewer than 48 tones. Sticklers for law and order will probably maintain that the octave shift reduces the number to the same old twelve, but in doing so they will be overlooking the obscure role of the octave, in that it comes at different points in different tetrachords and is occasionally transformed into a minor ninth, a truly "Schoenberghian" interval. The octave both exists and is non-existent: it has been relativised and thus becomes possible to use, with new accidentals, thereby solving the compositional problem formulated above.

This ocean of tones is anything but desolate. On the contrary, there are a number of beacons imparting structure to it. We have already made their acquaintance, and by way of conclusion they will again be placed at the centre of things. We recall Leibniz's thought of music as secret mathematical exercises for the soul, and Handschin's commentary that Leibniz is here referring to the contemplation of proportions, i. e. the interrelationship of tones manifested in intervals. We further recall that Handschin also emphasises the other aspect of music, the emotional and subjective, and that this state of tension as being fundamental to musicology and the philosophy of music. We can now add: and for artistic creativity as well. The composer must all the time relate to the fact of working with a material which, in purely musical terms, has certain given preconditions. The proportions can be questioned and attacked, parodied and abused without their fundamental standing being seriously jeopardised, based as they are both on man's own psyche and on external reality. Composition becomes a representation of this antithesis, with beauty resulting from the contest between the subjective and the objective, given. Composition becomes drama.

Tone and Meaning

"Music hath the power of making heaven descend upon earth". Thus Charles Darwin, in *The Descent of Man*, himself quoting a dictum from ancient China. The same words recur in Denis Dutton's *The Art Instinct*, p. 213, a work which seeks to anchor the practice and experience of art in ancient human adaptability. The perspective is anthropological, and art is by no means a product of later developments in high civilisations. On the contrary, it responds to human needs of building worlds of our own, a need which cannot always be viewed solely as a strategy for survival. It is a stage of evolution and humanisation and as such of vital importance to our self-image. According to the book's title, art has the character of an instinct which plays a dominant role in our lives. The author of the present essay is by no means foreign to that way of seeing things, based as it partly is on references to the dawn of history, albeit mythically garbed. And so there is cause to dwell for a moment on some of Dutton's trains of thought, especially those shedding light on tone and, with it, music.

One of Dutton's fundamental thoughts is that "the artistic instinct" goes back to man's experience of the Pleistocene era, i. e. the period from about one-and-a-half million years ago to the latest ice age. Man's "ur-landscape" was presumably the savannah, and from there he has carried with him criteria of what he considers to be beautiful natural scenery: meadows of waving grass, rounded hills, scattered copses with a lake glittering in between. These criteria of beauty have the character of an idyll and a possible musical counterpart in the Darwin quotation above, in which music, we read, "arouses in us various emotions, but none the more terrible ones of horror, fear rage, etc. It awakens the gentler feelings of tenderness and love, which readily pass into devotion". One can imagine a soundscape of birdsong and the wind whispering through the treetops and man endeavouring, with the aid of tone and its relation to other tones, to recreate this – a fictitious idyll, so to speak, with great impact and with fundamental traits of its own as I have previously described them with reference to interval selection.

More specifically, Dutton addresses our senses and their importance for the development of art. This he does in Chapter 9, headed *The Contingency of Aesthetic Values* (pp. 203–219). He asks why the sense of smell has not, like the sense of hearing, become the vehicle of a richly developed art. After all, both senses are equally good at distinguishing stages or components of each manifestation – hearing tones and rhythms, the sense of smell fragrances and odours. The latter, not least, has at its command innumerable nuances and transitions between them. Perhaps that is the problem and part of the explanation why the sense of smell has not been elevated to an art; Aleksander Skryabin's dreams of a *Gesamtkunstwerk* in which fragrances would be an integral part can presumably be taken as an exception. The sense of smell is of course an outstandingly important factor for human survival, perhaps even more so than hearing. And yet it has been of no consequence of artistic instinct, and this has been due to its various components not being amenable to systematisation, not being demarcated in relation to one another. As we all know, quite the opposite applies to the world of sound and, accordingly, tone, as witness, not least, our earlier discussion of scale and glissando. To this is added another important circumstance underscored by Dutton: music is an art of repetition and memory, and the mere thought of introducing a recapitulation in the world of fragrance/odours is unthinkable. Music's repetition extends from the small – a phrase or a section – to the very biggest: wanting to hear a long composition again, no matter how familiar it maybe, after a number of hearings, which has to do, not with a particular interpretation but with the composition in itself. The very memory of the music serves as a catalyst for listening to it again, at the same time as we can hum or whistle parts of it to ourselves or recreate episodes within ourselves. We recall Augustine's description of the role of memory in the experience of time by repeating a psalm: " Before I begin, my attention encompasses the whole, but once I have begun, as much of it as becomes past while I speak is still stretched out in my memory. The span of my action is divided between my memory, which contains what I have repeated, and my expectation, which contains what I am about to repeat. Yet my attention is continually present with me, and through it what was future is carried over so that it becomes past." (Tr. Albert C. Outler, cf. Bucht: *Rum – rörelse – tid*, p. 21).

The image of music which Dutton conveys is dynamic: in an evolutionary perspective, nothing is foreordained: it is coincidence that decides the direction to be taken by both prehistory and history. Darwin's notion of music's ability to arouse both soothing and ecstatic feelings is admittedly appealing, but it is not certain that this has always been the case or will be the case in future – given the background of the play of coincidence. Music contains so many possibilities and tone is charged with meanings. These will now be placed at the centre of attention, with some reversion to earlier chapters and the discussions contained in them.

* * *

Let us start with the discussion that has taken place concerning the difference between speech and singing. We found that they have one thing in common, namely pitch, as witness the human voice. The difference between them lies in the treatment of pitch – modulating in speech, focusing in song. But this distinction leaves room for intermediate positions, one of them being the *Sprechgesang* cultivated by Arnold Schoenberg, a procedure apparently inspired by the contemporary way of reciting a text. A completely different intermediate position might exist in Gregorian chant. According to Michaela Kohlhaas, the terms *cantare*, "sing", and *dicere*, "say", are used without the boundary between them needing to be absolutely clear-cut. Thus the latter term can also mean tones sounding, while the former refers more clearly to tone, sometimes expanded to include instruments. The whole thing is connected with Gregorian chant being borne up by the word and its message. The tone is in the service of the word, and the terminology is adapted accordingly (*Musik und Sprache im gregorianischen Gesang*, pp. 66–67).

A third parallel, if not intermediate position, between speech and song is to be found in Denis Dutton's *The Art Instinct*, pp. 214–215. Starting with a comparison of Darwin's between a speaker, a bard and a musician, Dutton points to a congruence between speech and song: "Song – speech rhythmically expressed in pitched tones – is universal and obviously the simplest musical form. But there is an important feature instrumental music also shares with language, a feature that tends to go unnoticed. The language-recognition machinery of the human brain fundamentally distinguishes vowel sounds – pure, simple tones – from consonants, which are more complex, and combined with vowels create a gigantic realm of linguistic possibility. This enables us not only to distinguish human speech from other noises but to make countless subtle aural differentiations, not only with the singing voice but in instrumental music as well. Musical pitches are the equivalent of vowels – 'super-vowels', they have been called – that stand in systematic relation to each other: the fifth, the octave, diatonic tuning and so forth. The attack of an instrumental note, the first tenth of a second or less, is picked up by the ear in the way that a consonant at the beginning of a word is acoustically perceived; it conditions how its vowel is heard: the acoustic differences between the spoken "play" "bay", "day" and "stay" are minute, happening in the first milliseconds of the words. Anyone who has played with digital editors or even magnetic tape may know that, in exactly the same way as removing the consonant, snipping off the attack of a note can make it impossible to distinguish whether it is being played by an oboe or a violin or a clarinet".

This passage demonstrates with abundant clarity how speech and song, word and tone, have certain properties in common, properties crucial to the kind of word and the kind of tone we hear. But this does not affect the fundamental difference between word and tone, speech and song, nor does Dutton claim it to. We are still in no doubt about these two phenomena, all their similarities notwithstanding, belonging to separate worlds in which reciprocal illumination has the task of getting to know them better as unique phenomena, each in its own right. To this end we shall once again call upon Plato, in order to track down other essential aspects with the aid of his systematisation.

"What should philosophy address, if not *the thing itself* – not its depictions and shadows, not its representatives and ostensible guises, but itself, in its identity and similarity to itself?" This is the opening sentence of a lecture delivered by the Swedish philosopher Sven-Olov Wallenstein and entitled *Platon och saken själv* (Plato and the Thing Itself, kindly placed at my disposal by the author). To me there is a striking connection here with the theme of the present book, namely what a tone is or can be – or, in Kantian terms: *der Ton an sich*. The notion of "the thing itself" has a long philosophical history, concretised in more recent times not only by Kant but also by Hegel, Husserl and Heidegger. But the story begins with Plato, who coined the expression "the thing itself", *to pragma auto*. What is this thing? According to Plato, there are necessary steps to knowledge: name, definition, image or sensory copy, knowledge and – the fifth and final step – the thing itself, "the purely existing". An example from geometry will serve to illustrate this train of thought: the name is the circle, definition is that which has distance from outer points to centre, sensory copy or image is when we draw and erase. Out of these three knowledge is born which comes close to the fifth and final step: the thing itself. This last mentioned is difficult to put into words, at the same time as the way to is passes through language.

Another approach disregards the ontological character, preferring instead to see "the thing itself" as the result of an interpretation. In Wallenstein's words: "It is a hieroglyph whose meaning can never be anything but a chain of names, definitions and images which at one and the same time projects an outermost anchorage point and takes it away from us." Thus viewed, "the thing itself" would be a *fata morgana* or a kind of pretext for asserting that one has been contemplating ideas. It would thus be an expression of philosophy's own ambitions and self-image, "its idea of its own truth".

All that has now been said can be seen as a problematisation of *the word* and its capacity for arriving at "the thing itself". In a summer programme broadcast on Swedish Radio on 22nd July 2007, someone quoted a dictum of Paul Valéry's which is pertinent to our discussion: "The word can be walked over but not stood on." Which is to say, in an ongoing presentation the meaning of the words is clear, but if we pause to contemplate individual details, their meaning eludes us. Let us test the same formulation on the sphere of tone: "The tone can be walked over but not stood on." Is this so? In an ongoing presentation, i. e. where tones are combined with each other, their (specific) meaning is clear, but if we pause to contemplate one single tone, its meaning does not by any means elude us, for the simple reason that, in principle, that tone can be sustained indefinitely. It can be charged with meanings, as happens in the sections of Alban Berg's *Wozzeck* and Ingvar Lidholm's *Poesis* which we were considering earlier on, not to mention the music of Giacinto Scelsi and the repertoire for the ancient Chinese *ch'in*.

In order to come closer to the meaning of a tone, it may be worth while testing Plato's five-stage method: the name is tone, the definition is a form of sound with a harmonic oscillation, a sensory example occurs when we pluck a string, set a column of air in motion or press the button of electronic apparatus. These three steps give birth to the fourth – meaning and knowledge – which in turn is ever so near the fifth step, the tone itself. Is its meaning elusive, do we lack tools for showing, with the aid of language, what a tone *is*?

In Chapter 1, p. 15–17, I discussed the tone-speech relation and its implications for our perception of tone and its properties. A quotation from the Danish composer Carl Nielsen sheds further light on what a tone is or can be: "(...) we are free to imagine the fresh wonderment and joy the first human beings may have felt at the sound of a taut string or the tone from a pipe or a horn which they tried to blow air through. What a feast it must have been!" (*Levende Musik*, p. 47). Nielsen puts his finger on a decisive point: the tone as the focal point of our attention and a specific meaning allied thereto. Granted that primitive man was surrounded by a soundscape in which tones were included; the discovery and experience of a concentrated moment of listening to a tone is nevertheless qualitatively different. Man experiences the tone in itself and is transported to another world with other preconditions and norms. The experience is like a flash of lightning, a revelation, as one also senses in the ancient myth, quoted by Handschin, concerning the origin of music. Something similar occurs in the above quoted example of vocal transition from speech to song. The tone wants something with us, but what? We have now come to a parting of the ways, i. e. the crossroads of choice between alternative angles of approach as presented by Sven-Olov Wallenstein: ontology or interpretation. In short: *Quid est tonus?*

Let us test a few answers concerning the ontological character of tone, i. e. what its basic meaning could be. In a previous work (*Quid est tonus?*, p. 145) I have argued that "tone is a miracle". On closer reflection, this seems an empty statement. No matter whether it is applied to the individual tone or to the interaction between tones, the word "miracle" is at one and the same time too vacuous and too comprehensive to be capable of pinning down "the thing itself". The word expresses our joy and wonder at the phenomenon of tone, but it adds nothing to our understanding of the phenomenon's meaning. There is so much in life that we could designate as miraculous: our evolution as a species, our lives, our capacity for transcendence, i. e. our ability to reach beyond ourselves. The experience of tone forms part of this complex but cannot lay sole claim to miracle status.

Chapter 1 of the present work ends with the following sentence: "If sound is the world, is tone the world's explanation?" (p. 30). This sentence is interrogative in form, but it could really be formulated as a statement. As such it reflects a fascination over the possibility of tone actually being an explanation of the world. In this way it follows on from a tradition which begins with the notion of the harmony of the spheres and could also be instanced with the present-day string theory concerning the nature of the universe. The world as one enormous harp with innumerable strings and tones – some vision! The only problem is: which world? It is evident from our exemplification that "world" means the universe, which begs the question of living conditions on any other planets which may be inhabited. They probably differ a great deal from our own living conditions, and so the sensible course is to let "the world" be identical with our own world, here on planet Earth, as it has evolved in the course of millions of years. That will be enough and to spare.

The above quotation – about tone as an explanation of the world – comes in a context where both Friedrich Schlegel and Robert Schumann seem to be asserting that this is really the case. Are we to believe them solely on the strength of the beautiful wording and its accompanying music, or must we, our aesthetic delight notwithstanding, soberly test the proposition's truthfulness? "Tone explains the world" – could this be "the thing itself"? How is the world of tone explained: as a sustained, inaudible tone permeating existence, as an audible interplay between tones where, via the intervals, we audibly discern proportions, converting acoustic numeric relations into experienced euphony or cacophony? These questions seem to presuppose an answer which not only radiates aesthetic value judgement but also includes a certain measure of verifiability. Clearly, this is not possible. Even if our experience of the interplay of tones and its starting point in acoustic conditions appear to suggest something underlying, "something else" (Handschin), this other thing will not allow itself to be conjured forth. Instead of invoking this other thing, perhaps we should problematise the *musica mundana – musica humana* relationship, though it is unclear how. This leads us to realise that language frustrates the quest for tone as "the thing itself" and paves the way to our establishing that the basic meaning of tone is its existence.

Turning now to Wallenstein's second alternative – tone as a hieroglyph with a combination of meanings, " a chain of names, definitions and images which at one and the same time projects an outermost anchorage point and takes it away from us," as he puts it. Let us consider the term "anchorage point". This already crops up in the situation, familiar to concert-goers, of the orchestra tuning its instruments. The tuning tone is the anchorage point for the musicians' attention, but also a signal to the audience that things will soon start to happen, that not just one tone but masses of tones will sound. The anchorage point is also present when intervals are delimited in relation to intermittent and ambient silence, as when various scale systems are presented, anchorage points against the threat of chaos materialised in *glissando*. The myth's fantasy about the first human being's encounter with tone puts perhaps even greater emphasis on its character of focal point, at the same time as an active, not only contemplative trait makes itself felt: the tone seems to be trying to tell us something, begging our attention. We respond to this exhortation by seeking other tones and combining them. In doing so we touch on the ability of tone to reproduce itself, expansion seems to be a part of its meaning, it seems, while in its cradle, to contain all the world's tones and thus music. The enumeration of different meanings could doubtless be extended, but one conclusion appears unavoidable: tone is the sum total of its meanings.

In Denis Dutton's *The Art Instinct*, a whole chapter, headed *The Uses of Fiction*, pp. 103–134, is devoted to the importance of narrative for human development. Storytelling seems to have developed early as an adjustment to ambient conditions and as a means of coping in one's imagination, with problems occurring in "real" life. The situation, of course, is supremely social from the beginning: people sit round a fire and one of them tells a story which could be true but is nonetheless invented or handed down from earlier generations. The combination of reality and fantasy is a distinguishing characteristic of such narratives, and therefore they are of concern to us, they teach us to lead a life with a dimension of depth, even if, following the invention of writing, the social component does not play the same role as it used to.

One is readily moved to ascribe tone, and with it music, the same role in the development of our humanity. A more or less straight line can be drawn from prehistoric gathering round the camp fire with singing and dancing, the playing of instruments to enthusiastic listeners/participants, to present-day pop galas and concert halls. Persons attending such arrangements do so with the express intention of listening to tones and rhythms, i.e. music, together with other people. Here again, the social component has been weakened by the development of musical technology and consequent at-home listening, but not to such an extent as to seriously impair the force of music. Its importance stands forth as undiminished.

Music aesthetics has agreed that tone and music can convey feelings. But can they tell a story? Do they have the same importance for man's adaptation of Life as the spoken word? At all events, the different meanings of tone as they have now been described do not appear to exclude a narrative character, though the narrative points more to the contrast between movement and repose, between light and shade, than to a more specifically, semantically established content. Whatever its survival value, tone appeals powerfully to our fantasy and is of value to us, which leads us to the following conclusion:

With tone we build ourselves narratives of space, movement, change and time.

References

Bodin, Lars-Gunnar:	*Musiken – en gränslös konstart?* (Music – a Boundless Form of Art?). Nordisk Estetisk Tidsskrift (The Nordic Journal of Aesthetics) nr 27–28 2003.
Bollnow, Otto Friedrich:	*Mensch und Raum.* Stuttgart 1963
Bucht, Gunnar:	*Europa i musiken* (Europe in Music), Stockholm 1996
Bucht, Gunnar:	*Rum, rörelse, tid* (Space, Movement, Time). Stockholm 1999
Bucht, Gunnar:	*Pythagoras' sträng* (Pythagoras' String), Stockholm 2005
Bucht, Gunnar:	*Rum, människa, musik* (Space, Man, Music). With a CD attached. Stockholm 2009
Bucht: Gunnar:	*Quid est tonus? Jacques Handschin, Der Toncharakter – och därutöver* (Jacques Handschin, Der Toncharakter – and further). With a summary in German. Hedemora 2009
Davies, Stephen:	*Themes in the Philosophy of Music.* Oxford University Press 2003
Dutton, Denis,	*The Art Instinct.* Oxford University Press 2009
Filosofilexikonet	(Dictionary of Philosophy). Stockholm 1988
Goehr, Lydia:	*The Imaginary Museum of Musical Works.* Oxford 1992
Goehr, Lydia:	art. "Philosophy of Music". I. Introduction, 1. A sceptical beginning. *The New Grove's Dictionary of Music and Musicians,* 2 ed. 2001

Handschin, Jacques:	*Der Toncharakter. Eine Einführung in die Tonpsychologie.* Zürich 1948. (Reprint Darmstadt 1995)
Handschin, Jacques:	*Musikgeschichte im Überblick.* Luzern 1948
Handschin, Jacques:	*Über reine Harmonie und temperierte Tonleitern* (Ausgewählte Schriften. Herausgegeben und eingeleitet von Michael Maier. Schliengen 2000
Jammer, Max:	*Concepts of Space. The History of Theories of Space in Physics.* With a foreword by Albert Einstein. 3rd ed. New York 1993
Kivy, Peter:	*Platonism in Music* from *The Fine Art of Repetition.* Cambridge University Press 1993
Knepler, Georg:	*Geschichte als Weg zum Musikverständnis.* Leipzig 1977
Kohlhaas, Michaela:	*Musik und Sprache im gregorianischen Gesang.* Beihefte zum Archiv für Musikwissenschaft, Band 49, Stuttgart 1991
Langer, Susanne K.:	*Feeling and Form.* London 1953
Maier, Michael:	*Jacques Handschins "Toncharakter". Zu den Bedingungen seiner Entstehung.* Beihefte zum Archiv für Musikwissenschaft, Band XXXI. Stuttgart 1991
Nielsen, Carl:	*Levende Musik* (Living Music). Copenhagen 1947
Reti, Rudolph:	*Tonality, Atonality, Pantonality.* London 1958
Ridley, Aaron:	*The Philosophy of Music. Themes and Variations.* Edinburgh University Press 2003
Schaeffer, Pierre:	*Traité des objets musicaux.* Paris 1966
Schopenhauer, Arthur:	*Die Welt als Wille und Vorstellung.* Ed. München 2002
Scruton; Roger:	*The Aesthetics of Music.* Oxford University Press 1997

Strindberg, August:	*Röda rummet* (The Red Room).1879
Strindberg, August:	*Stora landsvägen* (The Big Highway). 1909
Vogel, Martin:	*Schönberg und die Folgen. Teil 1: Schönberg.* Bonn 1984
Wagner, Richard:	*Mein Leben.* München 1969
Wagner, Cosima:	*Die Tagebücher.* München 1977
Wallenstein, Sven-Olov:	*Platon och saken själv* (Plato and The Thing Itself) 2008, unpublished
Wallrup, Erik:	*Musikaliska hemsökelser. Etyder om musik.* (Musical Visitations. Studies in Music). Stockholm 2002
Weber, Max:	*The Rational and Social Foundations of Music.* Carbondale, III 1958 (German orig. *Die rationalen und soziologischen Grundlagen der Musik.* Appendix to Wirtschaft und Gesellschaft, Tübingen 1921–22
Wiggen, Knut:	*De två musikkulturerna* (The Two Cultures of Music). Stockholm 1972
Zuckerkandl, Victor:	*Sound and Symbol.* New York 1956 (German version *Die Wirklichkeit der Musik.* Zürich 1963)

Index

Adams, John 100
Adorno, Theodor Wiesengrund 35, 37
aeolian harp 32
akousma/acousmatic 12
Aristotle 15, 48f.
Aristoxenus 15

Bach, Johann Sebastian 75
Bartók, Béla 25, 27f.
Beethoven, Ludwig van 15, 21f., 82
Berg, Alban 80, 108
Berlioz, Hector 32, 59
Blomdahl, Karl-Birger 64
Boethius 28f., 35, 37
Bollnow, Otto Friedrich 48, 58, 68
Brahms, Johannes 32
Brentano, Franz 17
Bruckner, Anton 21, 23f., 27, 68, 81f.
Bruno, Giordano 73
Bücher, Karl 33

Cage, John 11
Campanella, Tommaso 46
character of tone 37, 73, 109
ch'in 83ff., 108

Cowell, Henry 32

Dali, Salvador 51
Darwin, Charles 17, 33, 103
Davies, Stephen 36
discovery/invention 89f., 92
Dutton, Denis 103, 106, 111

Einstein, Albert 50
Euclid 50

fiction 111
flowing room/space 70
Fragmente-Stille. An Diotima (Nono) 77

glissando 27f., 76, 95, 104, 111
Goehr, Lydia 34, 37, 93
Goethe, Johann Wolfgang von 54
Gurney, Edmund 17

Handschin, Jacques 17f., 32, 37, 69, 82, 98, 101
Hanslick, Eduard 35, 37, 58
Hegel, Georg Wilhelm Friedrich 107
Heidegger, Martin 107
Helmholtz, Hermann von 17f.

Henry, Pierre 12
Hindemith, Paul 35
Honegger, Arthur 13
Hornbostel, Erich von 17
Hölderlin, Friedrich 77
Husserl, Edmund 107

Jammer, Max 48, 51, 58

Kant, Immanuel 88, 107
Kivy, Peter 92
Kohlhaas, Michaela 105
Köhler, Wolfgang 17

Leibniz, Gottfried Wilhelm von 43, 47 ff., 102
Lélio ou le retour à la vie (Berlioz) 32
Lidholm, Ingvar 79, 108

Mach, Ernst 70 f.
Mahler, Gustav 48
Messiaen, Olivier 15
Mitropoulos, Dmitri 100 f.
Moses and Aaron (Schoenberg) 46, 96, 98
Mörike, Eduard 32
Musica Enchiriadis 101
Music for Strings, Percussion and Celesta (Bartók) 25
musique concrète 12, 19

Newton, Isaac 49
Nielsen, Carl 75, 108
Nono, Luigi 77

notation 37, 65 ff., 83 f., 88 ff.
Notre Dame, music of 66, 85, 91 ff.

Parsifal, prelude (Wagner) 26, 43
Plato 77, 90, 93, 107 f.
Platonism 46, 49, 89, 92
Poesis (Lidholm) 79, 82, 108
Prague Symphony (Mozart) 99
proportion 29, 37, 43, 85, 87, 102, 110
Pythagoras 12, 21, 29, 30, 35, 37, 52, 58, 64 f., 68, 72

Rameau, Jean-Philippe 9, 92
Ridley, Aaron 36
Riemann, Hugo 17
room/space, in general 88
room/space, in music 57, 59, 61 ff.
Russell, Bertrand 48

Scelsi, Giacinto 82, 84, 108
Schaeffer, Pierre 12, 19
Schiller, Friedrich von 92
Schlegel, Friedrich 30, 110
Schoenberg, Arnold 46, 51, 80, 95 ff., 100, 105
Schopenhauer, Arthur 35, 38–42
Schubert, Franz 54, 56
Schumann, Robert 30, 110
Scruton, Roger 67 f., 88
Sibelius, Jean 48

Sinfonia espansiva, beginning (Nielsen) 75
Skryabin, Aleksander 104
Socrates 77
Spencer, Herbert 17, 33
St. Augustine 104
St. Matthew Passion (Bach) 75
Stockhausen, Karlheinz 60
Stravinsky, Igor 75
Strindberg, August 14, 41
Stumpf, Carl 17
Symphony no. 9, beginning 1st mov (Bruckner) 23
Symphony no. 9, beginning 3rd mov (Bruckner) 23
Symphony no. 5, end 3rd mov (Sibelius) 120
system of fifths 23–27, 101

The Rhinegold, prelude (Wagner) 108

tone/rhythm 95
tonos 45, 47

Valéry, Paul 108
Vogel, Martin 95
void 45, 47

Wagner, Cosima 42
Wagner, Richard 26, 41
Wallenstein, Sven-Olov 107, 109
Webern, Anton 11
Wolf, Hugo 32

Xenakis, Yannis 51

Zarlino, Gioseffo 19
Zeno 47, 71
Zuckerkandl, Victor 69–72, 94f.

www.ingramcontent.com/pod-product-compliance
Ingram Content Group UK Ltd.
Pitfield, Milton Keynes, MK11 3LW, UK
UKHW041414180426
11947UKWH00007B/131